SHIFT HUMANITY

NAVIGATING YOUR INNER WORLD TO GENERATE POSITIVE SOCIETAL IMPACT

GRACELYN SORRELL

SHIFT HUMANITY

Copyright © 2025 by Gracelyn Sorrell

All rights reserved.

This book or any portion thereof may not be reproduced or used in any manner whatsoever without the express written permission of the author except for the use of brief quotations in a book review.

Unless otherwise noted, all Scripture taken from the Holy Bible, New International Version®, NIV® Copyright ©1973, 1978, 1984, 2011 by Biblica, Inc.® Used by permission. All rights reserved worldwide.

Also used: Amplified Bible (AMP), Classic Edition, Copyright © 1954, 1958, 1962, 1964, 1965, 1987 by The Lockman Foundation.

Also used: The Holy Bible, English Standard Version. ESV® Text Edition: 2016. Copyright © 2001 by Crossway Bibles, a publishing ministry of Good News Publishers.

Also used: The King James Version (KJV), public domain.

Also used: the New King James Version®. (NKJV) Copyright © 1982 by Thomas Nelson. Used by permission. All rights reserved.

We are not to use knowledge as a weapon, but rather as a resource to build people up. My hope is that you experience life in a new, edifying, life-giving way through these words that hold life. I write to you with hope that these words make your day bright, your heart leap with joy, and your soul prosper.

—Gracelyn

TABLE OF CONTENTS

DEDICATION

INTRODUCTION
YOU'RE MADE FOR MORE (SELFLESS SUCCESS)

SEASON 1: BLACK
INCUBATED PURPOSE (DEVELOPING YOUR INSIDE WORLD)

SEASON 2: PURPLE
AUTHENTIC IDENTITY (RECOGNIZING THE WORLD IN YOU)

SEASON 3: PINK
THE DEPTH OF LOVE (EXPERIENCING AUTHENTIC LOVE)

SEASON 4: RED
A YIELDED LIFE (THE URGENCY IN YIELDING)

SEASON 5: GREEN
HUMAN NATURE (EFFICIENT TO GROW)

SEASON 6: YELLOW
JOY COMES IN THE MORNING (ALIVE IN CHRIST)

SEASON 7: ORANGE
THE HEART'S FIRE (HEALING THE WOUNDS)

SEASON 8: GRAY

THE FOG IN FAITH (ANXIOUS FAITH)

SEASON 9: BLUE

CONTENTMENT IN THE CURRENT (AWAITING JOY)

SEASON 10: WHITE

THE PURE IN HEART
WITH NO ILLUSTRATIONS, NO FLUFF, AND NO PERFECTION

FINAL REFLECTION

ACKNOWLEDGMENTS

NOTES

Dedication

I dedicate *Shift Humanity* to my late father, who I had for fourteen beautiful years, who inspired the colors of my life and ignited my glow.

And I dedicate this book to you. If you're reading this, you were meant to. You're right here, right now, for a reason. If you were ever unsure about your purpose in life, rest assured that you haven't missed the mark. Your breath today tells me that you're capable and purposed. What if I told you that the fatherless have a father? What if the ones who have an earthly father have a dad but not a God? What if what you lack is temporal and awaiting something deeper? This book is dedicated to the one who has a father but not a friend. To the one who has been disciplined but not discipled. To the one who has been abused but not held. To the one who has been improperly loved. To the one who's skeptical of love. To the one who is looking to fill an empty heart. To the one who doesn't see the purpose in their place. To the one who doesn't understand the masterpiece that they are. Come and dive into the events of life with me. Let's discover reason through the seasons. I desire to bring clarity to your identity, hope to your hopelessness, and light to the darkness. We will cry through the tension, smile through the pain, laugh without fear, and uncover the reason for it all. My reason for writing is for your longing to be embraced, your emptiness to be filled, your unknowns to become known, and your darkness to become light.

And to the little girl who was told she'd be an author at eleven years old and thought it would be impossible—Gracelyn, look at what you've done with pain. Remember that little girl who always wanted to see what you'd do with today. Persist.

Introduction

You're Made for More (Selfless Success)

For a revolutionary world change, all you have to do is be. You actively change the world through your actions, responses, and perspectives. You matter more than you might think, and your individuality creates unity once expressed. *Shift Humanity* is a creatively heartfelt journey of authentic seasonal lessons that yield joyous, purpose-filled, hopeful living that impacts the world. *Shift Humanity* gives us perspective on how our responses and actions shape the world *in* and *around* us, creating dynamic societal impact. Consider this book to be my written, colorful heart—a tapestry of arranged seasons creating a work of art for hearts and homes beyond my own. My stories are developed life lessons that are now a safe place for the one who desires to glow and grow through the challenges of a yielded life. Each chapter is a color, each color is a season, and each season is one in which we can live with optimal hope, joy, peace, and love. My goal is to help you navigate the "how" through the challenging, seemingly impossible seasons.

I have found there to be a priceless glow that nobody can give and nobody can take away. This glow flows from an internal place that can take some digging to discover, but the joy is in digging together. As life can be an array of emotions, situations, and changes, we will navigate through the mundane and the chaos of life in a bright, unique, poetic, and colorful way. In every season, I express my heart through vulnerable personal experiences and the lessons learned. Fair warning: I will cover an array of different experiences involving loss, insecurity, addiction, love, discontentment, trauma, passion, and abuse. I do not write about these experiences to bring glory to the event but to elevate the One who deserves all glory, even in our most vulnerable places. If an event in your life is still raw, some seasons may be difficult to read. I encourage you to guard your heart, ask the Father for comfort, and even seek professional help if something is stirred within you that feels too difficult to navigate alone.

As challenging as seasons can be with an array of spectrums and strokes, I give language to our *entire* reason for living through defeat and how victory is accessible every time. Some sentences are like journal entries. Sometimes, in these journal entries, I refer to my late father and, other times, my heavenly Father. The contrast between loss and hope is why I am writing to you. I have hope that you, too, will experience newfound joy that lasts, despite the nuances and chaos that this wild life will inevitably bring to your canvas. You may grieve with me through the season *Black*, find joy with me through the season *Yellow*, love with me through the season *Pink*, and cry with me through the season *Red*. Throughout your journey of *Shift Humanity*, don't shy away from the very moments you're here to acknowledge. I'll showcase and introduce practical ways to live an internally content lifestyle that makes even the hardest battles worth fighting. I want to remind you of who you are and who you have the ability to become. Lean into the questions around the possible tension and feel the emotion within the vulnerability of each season. To every seemingly defeated beginning, there's *always* a victorious end.

Season 1: Black

Incubated Purpose (Developing Your Inside World)

Who would willingly give her life to a God who allows a fourteen-year-old child to watch her father die a slow, gruesome death? I still remember the heart-wrenching loss like it was yesterday. My beloved father was dying. How does that little girl comprehend the God she grew up serving Sunday to Sunday? In her perspective, God withheld His love because He took away her first love. This cannot be understood.

Our human experience brings many nuances that we don't comprehend. We understand that we have breath in our lungs, but in our lowest moments, the question becomes, "Why?" We become tired of loving, waiting, fighting, hoping, and dreaming, and it seems like life becomes a cyclical routine of less-than-desirable activities—pumping gas, grocery store runs, and unwanted commitments. Life is nothing like the Disney movies, and it surely doesn't have a fairytale ending. Disappointment often comes from spaces of hopelessness and attempted success. When life doesn't go as planned, we wonder if starting was even worth it. Was there a purpose in obedience? Was there a meaning to all the trials? Was the temporary pleasure even worth it? Was it worth the credit card swipe? We tend to make decisions based on instant gratification but rarely consider the long-term effects. It feels great in the moment, but then our decisions catch up to us, leaving our hearts in a space of depression and hopelessness. Then, hopelessness tends to make us feel like none of it was worth it.

At a young age, after my dad's death, I felt a strong sense to pursue a meaningful life; I just didn't know what meaning was. So, my question became: How do I live with meaning if I see no meaning? From age fourteen, I realized that there was something beyond me, pulling me toward it. Was it the universe, my consciousness, my parents' faith, or a God who wanted me? At the time, I had no answers, but I slowly discovered that my response to sorrow and pressure was God giving me an opportunity to draw near to Him. In hindsight, this was a God who was jealous, and wanted and desired to know me. At the time, *none* of it made sense. I felt like a broken canvas, like an art piece that would be left to dry and never purchased. The creative visionary in me desires the ability to *only* create and succeed, not grieve and question my entire existence throughout the process.

The reality is we create, we stumble, we try again, we fail, we get up, we climb, we cry, we come to our end, and *then* we succeed. When talking about success, some may sum it up as notoriety or the art of the hustle. When life is about the bigger picture, success becomes *completely selfless*. Success is the art of yielding our plans to the Maker of the schedule. True success requires three principles:

1. **Patient** *perseverance*

2. **Patient** *discipline*

3. **Patient** *endurance*

Do you notice a theme? Patience. Some would perceive success as quick, tangible, and material gain, but in my discovery, to have lasting success is to wake up and say, "Hey God, what's it going to be today?"—and then *relinquish control*. Success is in the simplicity of our yielded moments, but the only way to know success is to know the process of patience. Since I have dealt with grief and heart-wrenching loss, I now know the cost of living, giving, and growing. It's an interwoven tapestry. Giving God our days may not yield an *easier* life, but it does give us hope that success is produced in our most challenging moments, not in a temporary destination.

Life is like a detailed obstacle course. Imagine running through hoops of joy, climbing ropes of sorrow, and walking through mazes of contentment. Nothing is constant except what we *seek*. When the three principles of success become our routine, we understand that perfection is simply impossible and pain is inevitable. When we practice joy, we yield joy, attract joy, and pour that joy out. When our response becomes anger, we yield, attract, and pour out anger. The deep moments filled with unbearable sorrow and pain are the same moments that equip us with the tools we need to build a firm, grounded, lively life. Realizing this produces a shift in the world.

I now know that *life isn't fair*, and we will lose, but we will also win. There will be many seasons and moments lived that are contrary to our desires and plans. Life throws curve balls, and suddenly, we have no idea what we're doing, why we're doing it, or how we'll get through it. When we don't understand, we become reliant. Who and what we rely on shapes who and what we eventually become. The key to being shaped into the best version of yourself is to yield who you've always wanted to be and become open to the misunderstood trials that are woven into your story.

Heart of Gold

On a rainy suburban Illinois day, my mom, dad, two older brothers, and older sister were on an outing. I was sitting in the backseat, tucked in the comfort of the presence of family. It was a gloomy late afternoon with raindrops coating the car windows. A rainbow appeared in the sky, and my parents decided that we would follow the rainbow to reach the "pot of gold." At around seven years old, I pondered what it would be like to reach this "pot of gold," while realizing that my parents were cultivating space for their children to grow in imagination and wonder. I became curious about what was at the end and when we'd reach this treasure. I enjoyed the adventure, but when I figured out that there was no pot of gold, I had to use my imagination to discover what hope there was left to follow. This was an adventure that my parents created just so their children could be opened up to a life of *wonder*.

When did we lose our wonder? When did we stop dreaming? What power does the American dream have to cancel our wonder? What happened to the masterpiece that was inside of you before you lost that loved one? I'll tell you what happened to that fourteen-year-old girl when her daddy died; she died, too. Grief overtook me, and the years it took to bounce back are still upon me. Perhaps the pot of gold that we never reach is what we all face at one time or another. I believe God enjoys our wonder, and our desires never die, even when we feel we did.

In our human experience, we have hopes, dreams, wishes, and desires. I think I know what happens. As we grow in responsibility, we tend to default to survival mode. Our paycheck becomes priority, our school becomes our necessity, our home becomes our heaven, and our friends become our influence. We become far too comfortable with the life and lungs that were never promised to us. So, it's time to ask what it's all for. In our humanity, some have a mode that lives paycheck to paycheck, hoping that the cycle will end soon so that they can spend the rest of their lives in a mansion on the coast. This mode, if not altered, will continue from generation to generation. There's nothing wrong with dreams and desires, but recognizing that you are first called to be a change agent is the priority.

I'm grateful to have a mother who raised me to submit my will to God because better is one day with Him than a thousand anywhere else (Psalm 84:10). To offer some perspective, I consider *life* to be the "pot" and our decisions to be the treasure. We all hope that there will be a rich reward so we can feel like it was all worth it, but when you discover that the reward is the yielded life, you win.

> *My question to you is—if the prize is your yielded life, are you winning?*

For where your treasure is, there your heart [your wishes, your desires; that on which your life centers] will be also. (Matthew 6:21 AMP)

How tight are you holding on to the world, and how often do you live in *wonder*? There is a creator who created us to create and live in wonder regardless of how the world around us and the systems of the world operate. In every shade and season, we have a passionate call to know our identity, stand on truth, and navigate through all the many colors and ways of life. God does not play with your life, and He has made no mistakes with you.

We live in a time when anti-Christ beliefs are at an all-time high. The enemy's agenda is to thwart the plan that God has for you. For example, whatever is anti-Christ would attempt to pull you gently and far from what is a reflection of Christ. This agenda could present itself in your relationships, perspectives, responses, and heart posture.

> *It's easier to be bitter due to trauma than it is to be obedient when facing trials.*

Turning our backs to the light when darkness is around can tend to become a default. But how do we develop a heart that attracts light, exudes light, and pursues light? We do this by leaning into pure truth.

We can't endure hardship if we don't identify the truth. Truth does not apply to what you grew up understanding or believing but rather what you test and approve according to the Word of God (Romans 12:2). Not only does truth expose lies, but it also places us in a posture of *humility*. At times, symptoms of humility could feel like weakness, inferiority, and lack of confidence. But the truth about humility is it produces strength and purity, which, in today's world, if you are in pursuit of purity, you are an anomaly. We assume that strength only applies to those with a yielded life, but what if strength was created for the weak vessels who have *nothing*, yet *everything*? The truth is, the strong don't need strength; the weak do, and this is why I strive to boast in the Lord amidst my weakness, just as Paul did (2 Corinthians 12:8–10). There is strength in suffering and resilience in the middle.

In society, we celebrate the wins but forget that in God's kingdom, the win occurred before the finish line. You won when you tripped over the hurdle and prayed; you also won when you were the slowest runner but the most diligent trainer. We run this race of life for one reason, but most of us don't know why. For God to be Alpha and Omega is for God to know the beginning and end. To know this is to know that there is a plan of success that has already been established; it simply must be cultivated. Strength has no value if it's in our own power; eventually, self-sustained strength will break. It's okay to acknowledge that you are a broken, weak vessel in need of a strong, capable Savior. Your experiences, your loss, your family, and your lifestyle all play a role in the plan. Although those things do not define us, they all become what God uses to cultivate us.

The reward is in reliance. The gold is in the process. The light is in the yield.

You should only be concerned with two things:

1. Doing well.
2. Concluding well.

If none of life operates according to your liking, it's only as good as how you handle the tension. What are you exuding? What are you accepting? What questions are you asking God? When it never makes sense, how is it handled? Who do you run to?

There's a moment when we begin to sit in silence with who we are, who we were created to be, and *why* we exist. There comes a time when you come to the end of yourself, and you begin to find yourself desiring more out of your experiences and your love for yourself and the world. This is a point where you know there is more for you, and there is more *required* of you. You may feel a nudge, a pull, and an urgency for something higher. Embracing this spectrum of life is the art of desiring internal depth even when you don't understand the constant external pressure around you. What if I told you that you're on your way to making sense of dark seasons by yielding what you thought life would be? Do yourself a favor: Let go of your idea of who you've always thought you were and be consumed with what you are about to learn about the *new* you.

There is a *fine* art to the way that you have been created. It's time to discover the new you and yield the version of yourself that you thought you always knew. When we come to a point of optimal surrender, we come to a point of optimal self. There is a wonder, a fire, a passion, and a strength in you that will soon be revealed. There's a depth of knowledge that you will come into through this vibrant discovery of new life and victory. It's time to come alive; again, I say, it's time to come alive. As you read these stories and experience these spectrums, may you be overwhelmed with the peace of the Lord Jesus Christ. May you be consumed with truth as you read, may every word written be palpable, and may you see and experience the greatest love of all. May you urgently awaken to the truth and live in it daily. You are a domino effect. You are made for more; you are the pot of gold. It's time for you to *Shift Humanity*.

Negativity on Death Row

Now is the time to put negativity on death row and LIVE.

Incubate: to keep something safe and warm so that it can grow.

It's dark in the womb. At two pounds and one ounce, I fought to escape the place that I needed to be developed in. It was dark, dull, and depressing, so I escaped early on a Tuesday morning, June 29. I like to think that my strong fighting will is what got me here, but it was really the grace of God. Whenever my mom tells me my birth story, I'm in awe and wonder of God's grace toward mankind. Mom bled and bled before she birthed a high-risk baby; even doctors were shocked to witness my birth. Entering life was the first time I died. When we're born, we are entering a place that will produce more womb-like opportunities. We think life will go one way, but then it goes the opposite, in a seemingly downward spiral. We think we will get the job, then we don't. We think marriage will fix the issues of our dark childhood, but it only illuminates the darkness. We face realities that never match our desires, and we tend to reject our destiny because of this delay. When we enter this world, we enter strife, stress, and compounded opportunities that we must figure out how to handle regardless of who supports us or if we're still healing. It makes me think, why was I in such a hurry to get here?

In the incubator, I was processed to the extent of letting go and relinquishing full control, laying in a bassinet with jaundice, with just days until my possible death. I was only able to lay and wait until my destination was determined: death in the hospital or life in the world. My process not only affected me, but the questions of life or death rippled in the minds and hearts of those who awaited the determination. The incubator was a place of safety yet a place of uncertainty.

I have often been unable to enjoy life because I felt like I was back in an incubator—the place where everything goes black, and

I don't even know what it means to breathe. It's dark and warm yet oddly comfortable and familiar. The most painful places are the ones where we can't find language or proof of our existence because we can't see. When I'm finally released and born, I feel like I need to return to the space that formed me because I don't feel processed enough. The incubator of life is a place of uncomfortable safety, offering a world of the unknown as we remain monitored inside yet giving hope of where we could be headed if we remain faithful and still. Safety resides in the places of the unknown because it's the place where we no longer have a choice.

Making decisions is one of my most challenging tasks because I never want to steer my life in a direction that God never intended for me to go. Life is like this whole cycle of shining and hiding. You show up to have a highlighted, illuminated, bright moment—only for it to last but a breath. These are the questions that run through my head:

"If I experience light, is darkness soon to come?"

"If I experience dullness, will I ever get my color back?"

"Will this desert life ever drink water again?"

Fears and lies are only cycles of decision, but incubation is a choice we never had. When you're in a dark season, it can feel like it has lasted as long as you've lived. Darkness makes you feel like you've never seen light, encapsulated in the womb.

> *Womb encapsulation feels like defeat until you realize what's molding you was given to protect you.*

Development can feel debilitating, but the lack thereof can lead to death. I lived, yet it felt as though something in every season died.

Death to Self

On August 15, 2013, around five in the morning, with the dew barely awakened, my mom knocked on my door as the hallway light peeped into my room. I lay on the bunkbed, eyes already open as my mom gave the news: "The doctors just called Gracelyn; your dad just passed." I think I said something like, "Oh, really?" first processing how tired my underdeveloped body was on my first day of high school (I was what seniors called "fresh meat"). I asked a few questions like, "Mom, how are you?" and "Did you tell them"—meaning my siblings. My next thoughts were, "I will be okay, but I don't want anyone else not to be. Is everyone else alive? *Who will be taken next?*" That morning, my mom gave me the option to go to school or stay home. I went. If you know anything about the stages of grief, the first stage is denial.

I felt nothing about the information that was given. That morning, I got dressed in my first day of school outfit (because, in my head, impressing people was my top priority), and I headed into my new school in a complete haze.

Walking through the doors of what I knew would be a long four-year journey felt like the moment you're holding back tears, trying not to let them fall, resisting the urge to let anyone see your emotion. That entire year, I carried welled-up tears that never fell. I suddenly became "the girl whose dad died," not Gracelyn. There was no "How are you?" or "Is there anything you need?" and, of course, no "Can I pray with you?"

In my first class, the teacher asked how we were feeling on a scale of one to ten, and I was the only one who voted two. "Why ask if there would be no help?" I thought. Since my vulnerability was ignored and never addressed, I began to develop an internal mindset that nobody cared. Every response I've had throughout life's seasons became lifeless and dull—all because nobody seemed to care on that most important day. Apparently, I was just another student in a classroom who was there to learn, not heal. Society swallowed me up as I walked through the halls during passing periods. "Don't cry, don't cry," I thought. If I broke, so would my esteem. "I worked too hard on my first day of school outfit," I thought. Later that day, I came home, and my knees buckled in the driveway. Finally, there was safety to be broken. I was barely able to walk to the garage door when my mom met me and embraced me with deep, passionate warmth.

That was the year that I felt like I returned to the womb, where I was never fully developed. It was a year of lots of closed doors, escapes, "I'm not hungry," "Leave me alone," and a developed pornography addiction—all at the young age of fourteen. I felt like I would never escape this pit called life. "There was *more* of *this*?" I thought. How could I believe in a God when my own father wasn't alive long enough to believe in me? How could I forgive when my father never apologized for leaving his wife and children for months to years on end when he was alive? How could I believe a God who says He is love, yet He seems to forsake me over and over again? God, if You love me, deal with these tears. Deal with the wells of disappointment that I hold. If You care for me, I plead with You to take this pain away. God, if You wanted me to heal, then why are there marks and bruises left? They only leave dark spots. I never asked for residue. Facing dark seasons can cause us to question our existence. Yet, dark seasons were created to draw us *near* to God. He wants to show us that we can live through it—with *Him*.

Someone reading this feels surrounded by darkness. Maybe you feel hopeless and don't even have an explanation for it. I do:

> *You're supposed to be here. You're made to endure these moments. You can rise above opposition.*

In the dark hole of depression and doubt, my identity was undefined. Doubt is like the lost revelation of truth. When we lose our way, we're called to ask God to remind us of who we are. Although there were feelings of immense defeat, in the middle of the darkness, there was a sliver of hope that I clung to. It's the knowledge that I came to when my dad passed, and I wasn't left to figure it out on my own. I remembered my mother's subtle devotion, which was not always audible, but I saw the evidence of her faith lived out in front of me. Because of my mom's faith, I came to know that I, too, was left with a presence, a fragrance, a shadow, a Helper. God was not just the God of my mother but also the God who desired to know me. I wanted to know the God of my mother's soul and salvation. I desired the kind of relief that seemed to come during her worship in church. True friendship was revealed to me through my *curiosity* of God's nature. I believe one of the first steps we can take to increase our faith is to ask questions. Inquiring of God is not a sin; He *loves* our questions because He wants to communicate. God became the first *real* friend I ever had. When I realized that people couldn't fill my voids, I realized there was only one living hope. When my first love (my dad) left this earth, I found my true love, Jesus Christ, *Yeshua*.

When I was surrounded by darkness, a presence entered, and that presence had plans all along to sit with me in the dark and the mundane. Darkness causes *reliance*. Even though I found hope eventually, in the process, there were many times I sat fixed between darkness and light. It was as if I had a choice to walk into the addiction, sex, identity issues, fantasy, envy, anxiety, bitterness, anger, or invite the light in. In the darkness, there was *always* light, but I had to choose which one I would pursue.

After losing my dad, there were so many questions I had stored up. There was an internal switch that flipped that year. I realized that I couldn't see where I was going, so I would help make every dark path lighter if I could. I was torn on which way to go and couldn't put myself back together, so I turned to others. In the middle of mending other lives through my pain, I saw what I always desired—someone to love me like I loved them. Since I felt like I had lost everything, all I wanted was *something*, which is when I began to settle into defeat. We tend to invite destructive company when we're desperate. I became addicted to easing pain without God's love, which caused me to operate from a place of strife. Tolerating repetitive sinful behavior was my escape. Whatever I could get that felt like love, I held on to. I found the quickest and easiest way to cope through whatever felt good to me; nothing was off-limits.

This is what humanity does. We opt for the pretty thing over the valuable. Surely, pretty things can be valuable, but are they *beneficial*? We attract and become the things that make us *feel* good when only God knows what *is* good. This is why we surrender our will because the truth is, He knows you better than you'll ever know yourself. Once you know and understand the nature of God, you will know and understand what to do with the dull, mundane, dissatisfying moments. Temporal vices will not suffice for a thirsty soul. Premarital sex, money, non-biblical meditation, working out, and diets will not fulfill the soul. Nothing can quench a deep thirst like Jesus can. Until we *know* Him, we will often settle for the one who rubs our back and makes us feel the best, even if it's not good for us. My identity was met with the lie that all I had was all I'd lost, and I would never *be* or *have* anything more than lack and loss. However, in the midst of it all was a tiny speck of light that wanted me to see *and* wanted me. In loss, I still felt chosen. In lust, I still felt loved. Something was *fighting* for me. There are spiritual forces in the heavenly realm actively fighting against darkness for you. I now know this to be the Holy Spirit that Jesus left for us and the angels who wage war on our behalf. The Spirit was my Paraclete, my Helper, the God of angel armies desiring me the whole time. The God of my mother and father met me. The God that I saw through my mom's tears in church was after me, but I didn't know Him personally . . . yet.

When Darkness Caves In

For months before my dad's death, he was deathly ill. There were nights I would lay awake, wondering if my father would live until morning. At times, he became sick to the point of hospitalization, and doctors informed my mom that it wasn't looking good. My mom was dedicated to his care, which meant I sometimes spent nights away from home while she was tending to him. On one of these nights, while I wondered if my father was dead or alive, darkness rushed into the already black places of my heart in the form of sexual assault. Unwelcome lust arose as I lay there feeling helpless with someone else's desires being forced upon me at such a vulnerable time. Guilt and doubt washed over me—guilt that I was not with my dying father and doubt of the God that I'd just begun to discover. "*Was this my fault since I had fantasized about sex prior to the assault? Did I bring this on myself? Why would God allow this?*"

Years later, in therapy, I learned that just because I *thought* about it didn't mean I *approved* of it. I wanted to open the door of lust, but I *chose* to push my abuser off. We can have thoughts of defeat, but we are equipped with the authority to shut them down. Now I know that on that night, I didn't lose, I won. Second Corinthians 10:5 says we are "Casting down imaginations, and every high thing that exalteth itself against the knowledge of God, and bringing into captivity every thought to the obedience of Christ" (KJV). In that moment of darkness, just months before losing my dad to liver failure, I saw a street light. It was the only thing that was shining on the night of the assault. I was alone; where was I supposed to go? With tears rolling down my cheeks, I swallowed the reality that I was at fault, and my new life was one that consisted of a voiceless, meaningless, dead body in the flesh, lying ready to be preyed upon. I thought: *"This is all God's fault. The God of my mother and father failed me, and I'll do whatever it takes to be as far away from Him without disappointing Mom."*

A Reflection of Light

Darkness is deception, but without it, there's nothing to see. As I write to you, there is a new light shining in my window, and I see a reflection. A reflection of the time when the darkness reflected light—when the mirror reflected the brokenness that I felt, but it still never forgot that I stood there. A reflection cannot deny; a reflection cannot lie unless distorted by some outside force. Seeing light while feeling darkness is faith—even if the faith is small. What you see is what you reflect. My sight was distorted for about five years until I realized that even if I didn't understand why, I understood that the plan God had for me was not corrupt. *The plan that God has for you remains.* It's time to face the bare, ugly truth. What are your earliest memories of trauma, and how are you actively coping?

What we must realize is darkness is imagination. Seasons of darkness are an illusion to see what we will *do* with the cards that have been handed to us. It's not that God wants to see His children suffer; **He wants to be with us through it.** Suffering embodies eternal purpose beyond our knowledge. The daily choice of graceful surrender is the choice that shapes who we become. Graceful surrender is the art of leaning into a willing choice to relinquish control regardless of the outcome. Although I didn't choose to kick and scream the night of the assault, I was held by a grace that covered me to show that decades later, it would all be used for His glory. Don't be fooled; I'm still becoming the woman I dream of, but every day, I choose to be one or two steps closer to becoming one with God's dream for me.

It's time to become familiar with God's joy. There is no pressure to pass the test the first time. You fail, and you try again. You cry, you question, you seek answers, and you scream in feelings of defeat. Getting an F on the report card is not your label for failure; it is your call to *perseverance*. When you get an 'F' in life, you don't stop; you keep pressing until you pass that test. Years upon years later, in the middle of a brand-new dark season, I am reminded of the tests that I have only passed by God's grace and His grace alone.

Not only so, but we also glory in our sufferings, because we know that suffering produces perseverance; perseverance, character; and character, hope. And hope does not put us to shame, because God's love has been poured out into our hearts through the Holy Spirit, who has been given to us. (Romans 5:3–5)

> It is because of the LORD's lovingkindnesses that we are not consumed, Because His [tender] compassions never fail. (Lamentations 3:22 AMP)

In a blackout, the Holy Spirit takes us down the path that leads to God. He leads in such a way that prevents unnecessary falls; He lights the way, as a flashlight would in a dark space. Knowing the Holy Spirit is knowing light. Letting the Holy Spirit in is giving God permission to light up and guide your life regardless of how you wanted it to go. He exists to help you not waste time trying to turn on a light you cannot find. The Holy Spirit is perfect, but having the Holy Spirit does not mean that we are perfect. We will have to walk, ask, and make decisions, but now, our path is lit. We no longer need to trip over objects unnecessarily or fight our own battles. He gives us the strategy on how to respond to others (wisdom), who to respond to (discernment), and what to do about a particular scenario (guidance). With the Holy Spirit, you can prepare to "see" in a blackout. Spiritually speaking, pray and ask the Holy Spirit to lead you. Ask Him to interrupt your plans and then willingly trade your plans for His. He is the source and the Giver of light and life.

Maybe you're reading this, and you're a Christian—devout, saved, sanctified, and filled—or maybe you don't know Jesus at all, but we all need a reminder of who the Father is, where our hope is found, why we believe, and how to pursue Him. In the battles of life, our first response is usually one of the "flesh," but as we remember and understand who Jesus is, pursuing Him in every shade and season unlocks the meaning of what was once lost and powerless.

Pursuing the Light

Darkness is a muzzle. Darkness calls for *desperate* measures and extremes. You'd do anything to make the pain go away or to numb the pain. The question is, where do we go to get numb? For me, I would escape by watching pornography. As a fourteen-year-old girl, I began to think of what it would be like for my body to be desired. I wanted to know what it felt like to be wanted—not only feel wanted but BE wanted. God was amazing and everything to me, but He wasn't going to give me physical pleasure, so I went to the closest thing that I knew; I turned to hidden sin that would offer freedom.

It all started with YouTube. I was a young, curious girl looking up "how-to" videos and landed on "How to have a first kiss." Watching these videos became a daily routine, and eventually, I wanted more. I just wanted to feel desired. How-to videos turned into an addiction. I truly felt seen because I could imagine what it was like to be wanted by a false image of love that felt so real. Viewing pornography was my gateway drug, and all I wanted was relief to numb all the pain of self-image, loss, assault, and confusion. Imagine the feeling that you get when your own friends don't want to include you. Imagine that feeling when your body is never accepted by society. Imagine being that person who doesn't have that hair texture that's seemingly desired. Imagine being *different*. Maybe that's you. How does that make you feel? Probably isolated, worthless, overlooked, insignificant, and the list goes on. I truly had no escape from the pain that I felt every single day of my life. You might think, "How does a fourteen-year-old *girl* get involved in watching porn?" The same way one gets involved in drugs, alcohol, sex, binge eating, shopping, gossiping, fighting, or stealing. Satan uses *anything* that he can to derail us from God's plan, even the unconventional.

But it wouldn't last. Because even in the darkness, there was light. Even when I tried everything to destroy myself, God had other plans. It's time to be free from the tainted residuals of your past and thrive in the most authentic, originally created version of you. If I can do it, you can do it.

Season 2: Purple

Authentic Identity (Recognizing the World in You)

Identity issues don't stem solely from sexual trauma or lust; identity issues can stem from not knowing God, and they grow into a resistance to holiness. God is the resolve to all forms of confusion.

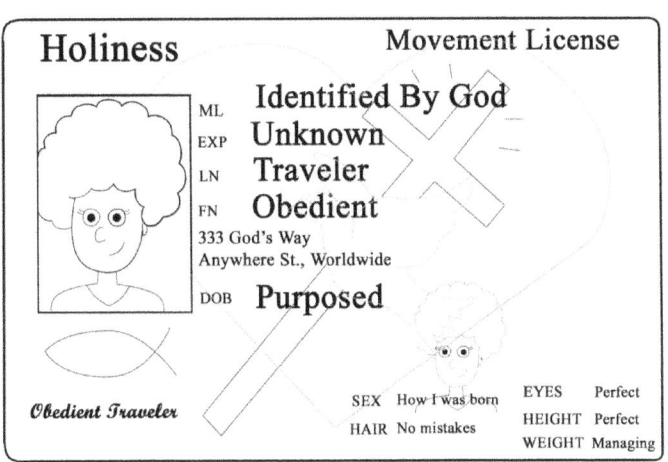

> But you are a chosen people, a royal priesthood, a holy nation, God's special possession, that you may declare the praises of him who called you out of darkness into his wonderful light. (1 Peter 2:9)

We are fashioned by God. We are knit and woven by His great love. His character is deep and vibrant. His speech is power and authority. His gentleness is lovely. He is kind. He is a gentleman who opens doors and closes them. He is the Protector. He is to be feared and revered. I just wanted to introduce you to the Father of grace, peace, mercy, forgiveness, and goodness. He's my best friend.

I am peculiar; I am loving. My voice can't get very loud, but my emotion can. I have been shy, but I'm breaking the barrier of fear and judgment. I am not picky; I am particular. One of my strengths is transparency; one of my weaknesses is insecurity. I care too much about what people say, but I am exceptional at strengthening my weaknesses. I *hate* glitter (unless it's sealed in something and unspreadable—in that case, it's very pretty). I love people but also struggle to love them. I enjoy music, I dance when I'm comfortable, I worry about little things because I care, and my name is Gracelyn. There's so much inside of me that I can't even begin to unpack in depth, but I notice that I couldn't be any of this without knowing *who* made me like this. My foundation runs deep. My identity is my foundation. My name, my face, my size, my weight; it's all a masterpiece and a work of art. But those things are not my identity; they are my features.

Sometimes, I look at the faces of others and think about what makes us different. Is it the size of our noses? The shape of our heads? The smile lines? We can all have the same features and the same sparkle in our eyes, yet we are so different. Shapes, sizes, *colors*. We all need the same things; we just get them from different sources. In discovering you, you must identify who you belong to and where you belong. Once you determine *whose* you are, then you can more effectively understand *why* you are. Why you act, sound, and look the way you do. If you belong to your parents, your security may be shattered because they aren't living. If your security is in your significant other, you may be broken because you gave yourself to them, exchanging yourself for the expectation of fulfillment. If you belong to your passion, you may feel empty because passion can only take you so far.

Maintaining something that runs out is a never-ending rat race.

Identity Cleansing

Baptism is not the only way to publicly display your vow to God; your *soul* must be cleansed from the wretchedness of your self-sustained identity. Oh, what a relief it is to know that man-made *religion* is contrary to what God has created. In the soul of the earth lies many gods (Allah, Buddha, Oshun, Satan, Sky god, Moon god, Greek gods, just to name a few), but you can only be identified by one. Maybe you've found peace but not fulfilling love. Maybe you found yoga but not internal wellness. Maybe you found power but not posture. You don't feel marked and designed, and it's because those gods didn't write your story; they plagiarized it. I'm not saying these deities aren't real; I believe they are, *but* there's a greater power. God is in all things because His nature made all things. He formed all of creation. The universe could never create your story. Maybe mold it, but never create it. Maybe you don't have *my* story, but you have *a* story—your uniquely woven story.

God uses so many avenues to reach us, and He reveals Himself to us all in different, unique ways that are catered to our identity. For example, there was a day when I was determined to write this book. I'd been frustrated for many months trying to write, but this particular Saturday, I was determined. A friend texted me, telling me that she'd made a cake and cut a slice for me. When we met up and I saw the cake, I was nearly in tears. She didn't know that I was writing a book of many colors. She didn't know that I was on my way to write away. She didn't know what I needed to remain inspired, but God did. This is the voice of God. I didn't hear a thing, but God sent a friend to present the message that I'm seen. What better time to bring me what's called "The Power of Sprinkles" cake?

Even better than you knowing yourself, you must know the God who knows you. This is how we determine His voice, His sound, and His communication style. He knows what you need when you need it. He knows where you're going and what you are going to do. He knows when you sit and when you rise. He knows who you're going to cuss out before you do it, He knows that you're on the verge of cheating, He knows that you don't know yourself as well as you thought you would by now, He knows that your job doesn't pay enough, He knows how much tuition costs, He knows the weight of your responsibility, and He knows the pain that you have endured. *He knows.* When we work to know Him better than we know ourselves, He reveals who we are in Him, sending little sprinkles to cast out our doubts with certainty, reason, and a solidified way to live full of life and color. What a blessing to be known by the God of hope.

The Intricacy of Identity

My mom was twenty-one weeks pregnant when her complications started. She was suffering with pins and needles all down her blue veins. She said, "God, if this baby lives, her name will have Grace in it." She also said to God that Friday, "If this baby is not born by Tuesday, I give up." About ten minutes before one in the morning, on *Tuesday*, June 29, Gracelyn Sorrell was born. Doctors came flooding in to see the miracle. The doctors and nurses could not believe how I had so much breath in my lungs and how we both made it out alive. My life was proof that God fights for His children just as glitter sticks to the skin. I identify as *fought for*. I identify as protected, spared, and chosen.

> Regarding your previous way of life, you put off your old self [completely discard your former nature], which is being corrupted through deceitful desires, and be continually renewed in the spirit of your mind [having a fresh, untarnished mental and spiritual attitude]. (Ephesians 4:22–23 AMP)

I want you to take a moment to recall what you have been protected from (this could be a car accident, relationship, or unexpected health issue). What has God shielded you from?

On this day, God shielded me while my brother placed me in a toy bulldozer. It was all fun and games, but I didn't seem to agree! I just wanted freedom! Look at that face. The cries of baby G. Thankfully, no Gracelyns were harmed. ;)

Identity and Intimacy

The magnitude of worthiness you believe about yourself is the same magnitude that you will receive. Identity and love coexist. Loving yourself means that God's wisdom and your soul collide to make decisions, and your decisions shape you. Knowing this, *you have control over your every move.* You can now question humbly, "Is this person *worthy* of loving me?" "Beyond everything physical and pleasing, does this move compliment my entire life?" Personally, if I were to pursue or get into the wrong relationship, then the pursuit was pointless. Maybe you're thinking, "No, it's a lesson." Yes, but because God made it a lesson despite the poor decision. This is His grace, but it is not to be abused. When you know better, you do better, and now that you've read this, you know.

> *Mistakes don't have to be made when we have the self-control and knowledge to prevent them.*

It's in our nature to self-pity when we've made the same mistakes over and over. We begin to think we have an issue and become a victim of guilt. Truthfully, we don't have issues; we have decisions, and these decisions lead to either sin or sanctification. When will we surrender and *actually* change? This is not always a problem that you produced; it's a deal that needs to be broken off with the devil. It's called a stronghold. Sin is very real, and it can begin in the clean text messages with smiley emojis. It can begin when you think, "I'm just not good enough." Whether it's a person, place, or thing, the enemy's tactic is to defeat you even in your devotion because even he knows how much you contribute to humanity. To become victorious over this scheme, every move you make must be made in deep thought, in prayer, and in *wisdom*. Why? Because you matter that much. We do this by including Christ, leaving Him out of nothing, and consulting with Him in all things.

Relationships are not only made for comfort but also for the safety and well-being of the soul, which was created for a greater purpose beyond you. Many people want relationships but not the weight or responsibility that comes with them. This is true for your relationship with God, friends, family, spouses, and even pets.

The Scavenger Heart

To the ones who feel their identity was left behind with that high school fling, you are more than that. Be renewed. You are searching for something that can only be found in the presence of the Father. He will fill you up with a longing for Him. Will you be tempted? Yes. Will you want to risk it all because the moment is heated? Yes. Will you feel heavier than hot because of the weight of sin? Yes. Is there a way to conquer this? Yes.

> *Go on a scavenger hunt for your heart; discover your true identity.*

There may be brokenness in places that you've never seen. I noticed that temptation arose because I lacked confidence that God still knew me. Hebrews 4:15 says, "For we do not have a high priest who is unable to sympathize with our weaknesses, but one who in every respect has been tempted as we are, yet without sin" (ESV). There may be pieces of your heart left inside of someone else's. There may be empty parts that need filling. Identify. Search—*for you*. Where are you? Where did you drop off your morals? Hopefully, you now understand why I have died to myself. Why I have chosen to give up what I *wanted* for the sake of Jesus. Surrender is costly, but it pays to surrender your heart. Nothing is more valuable than your heart; protect it at all costs. Galatians 2:20 says, "I have been crucified with Christ. It is no longer I who live, but Christ who lives in me. And the life I now live in the flesh I live by faith in the Son of God, who loved me and gave himself for me" (ESV).

We must use wisdom in who we tell what, what we say, and what signs we give. Sharing with the wrong crowd can lead to destruction, but sharing with safe community leads to a life well-built. If we want to *Shift Humanity*, we must watch our every move and proceed with precision. To know God is to know the depth of decision. It's time to discern if your surroundings are speaking to the light inside of you or dimming your light.

Psalm 139:13–15 says: "For you formed my inward parts; you knitted me together in my mother's womb. I praise you, for I am fearfully and wonderfully made. Wonderful are your works; my soul knows it very well. My frame was not hidden from you, when I was being made in secret, intricately woven in the depths of the earth" (ESV). You are not your features or qualities. You are more than the labels. I wanted sex because I wanted validation; now, I desire sex because I desire to worship God in a way that pleases His design. We were created spirit and flesh. If you were only flesh, who would your spirit worship? If you never had a body, what would become of your soul? Who does your spirit belong to outside of this flesh? Royalty is in the deepest place of your identity. How you see, how you feel, what you think, and whose you are. How deep is your love for Jesus Christ? How far would you run to find Him? How passionate are you in pursuing His nature? Flee from the passions of your flesh.

> *We are not what we see in the mirror; we are who we serve in spirit-we're just renting this body.*

"So flee youthful passions and pursue righteousness, faith, love, and peace, along with those who call on the Lord from a pure heart" (2 Timothy 2:22 ESV).

My body is a secret that only one man will know. It is a sacred place. Is purity limited to sex? No. Is sex limited to pleasure? No. That's just the beginning. Purity is in who and what you're after, and it's only obtained in Christ because we were made to worship.

Let's be honest. What is your heart scavenging? What are you after? What do you want most right now?

_____

_____

_____

_____

If you're not after purity, holiness, or righteousness yet, it's okay. Sometimes, surrender takes some searching. Remember, it took me facing the truth to receive a better life. When I understood why I wanted sin, it opened my eyes to what I lacked, and when we see what we lack, we can identify what we long for. In order for the diamond to shine, it must be cleaned. Purging is simply part of the process of purification, and this is all needed to shine authentically.

Image and Identity

Who is in your ear? Who is affirming you? Who do you confide in? I remember my first boyfriend always affirmed my appearance. I realized that his compliments were my validation and my driving force. I only wanted to please him because if he loved me, I could love me. But when he cheated on me, half of me left with him. I was tied to his compliments and our passion, but when he cheated on me, I went searching for the missing piece of me that he had (which I'd given him). Making love to an idea makes way for danger. It's called *longing*. Sin begins with a thought, and a thought can turn into a longing. Longing can either lead to light or lack. "Then, after desire has conceived, it gives birth to sin; and sin, when it is full-grown, gives birth to death" (James 1:15).

When your heart is not fully dedicated to the Father, your heart is divided. It is shared with something that is just as important to you as God. The enemy's tool to keep you bound is to keep you conflicted between your desire for God and your desire for sin. This is why pursuing God and confiding in Him is imperative. You begin to *want* more fulfillment when you lack joy. You want something deeper than a routine Monday through Friday. When you know God, He reveals Himself to you, and this is the production of contentment. You begin to realize that you were created on purpose by the One who created all things and continues to work in creation. Our life's purpose IS to know Him, not to interrogate Him. I remember when I got serious about pursuing God at seventeen, and all my desires started to make sense—inspiring, speaking, writing, creating, traveling. I desired these things before, but when I gave God permission to breathe on them, the reason why they were there became evident.

If we were the author of our lives, we would dwindle into a daunting valley. To know everything is to know nothing. The more we know, the more we realize we know nothing at all because there's always *so much more*. This life would not be yours to see if God put you here to exist and not expand. You are *purposed* for this journey; you were *predestined* for what you are living through right now. You were thought of before you were known. Nobody but a perfect God can create living beings with active energy created to impact exponentially. I've been in the place where I wished I was the only person living so that I could have God all to myself, but the truth is, a selfish heart doesn't benefit. We exist to share. The world spins so we can give more of ourselves, becoming less self-aware and more service-aware. Our image is only as good as our humility. This is why body image subjects itself to the cross; Jesus' body was broken for you to reveal your beauty. Our image is a reflection of the cross, and if Jesus Himself became a man of no reputation, so can we.

> But [he] made himself of no reputation, and took upon him the form of a servant, and was made in the likeness of men: And being found in fashion as a man, he humbled himself, and became obedient unto death, even the death of the cross. Wherefore God also hath highly exalted him, and given him a name which is above every name: That at the name of Jesus every knee should bow, of things in

> heaven, and things in earth, and things under the earth. (Philippians 2:7–10 KJV)

I know that we all have a longing to be seen, known, and loved, but we already are. He is with us, for us, and in us if we have given Him access. If you have given yourself over to Him—your heart, your mind, your will, and your emotions—that's what gives you the opportunity to know Him as your Father with no reason to compare yourself to others. The best part is you have His full and undivided attention right now. You also have His full acceptance as you are. God knows the real you better than you can even begin to describe your strongest personality trait. You have every reason to love and appreciate your body, from the abs to the rolls, from the freckles to the pimples, from the thick to the slim, from the biceps to the "no ceps," from the stretch marks to everything in between. That's the shallow part of you, but He wants you to love that, too, and trust that His artistic ability is perfect and purposed. Although this body is simply a shell and a cage that we rent, we are to celebrate the body that was broken for our beauty. This is a call to live to be healthy, not haughty. It's time to begin again and uncover the intention behind your image. Your pinky toe has more purpose than your false lashes or tattoos. Your confidence is called to be rooted in Christ. Just a few years ago, I became weary of the added hair, piled-on makeup, and impression for validation. It was tiring attempting to fit the societal mold. If someone had a tattoo, I suddenly desired one. If long hair was trending, I suddenly wanted it. If piercings were desired, I wanted more. The world's race never ends, and the most authentic form of you is the one who pursues Christ over culture.

I want to remind you again what Psalm 139:13–15 says: "For you formed my inward parts; you knitted me together in my mother's womb. I praise you, for I am fearfully and wonderfully made. Wonderful are your works; my soul knows it very well. My frame was not hidden from you, when I was being made in secret, intricately woven in the depths of the earth."

For these reasons, we should not chase what we see outwardly in others. We are to pursue the light that is pure, good, bright, and true, according to God's design. It's time to take care of yourself in a way that benefits the world around you. Most would consider self-care as grabbing some ice cream, going out on a solo date, or watching your favorite movie. I'd like to suggest an alternative way to care for yourself.

Practical ways to care for you: Go out with your natural hair, use your real voice, lay down the addictions, skip the unhealthy snack, detach body obsession, apologize to someone, talk about your struggles, pursue God, and forgive yourself.

Spiritual ways to care for you: Sit with God, talk to God, and commune with God.

Knowing God and pursuing God are different. We're all in a process, but one can pursue God yet never know Him. There's a strong, necessary call toward knowing who the person of Jesus is and was, and learning Him for all of your days, *then living like Him*. At times, pursuing God feels like a chasing, but we don't chase what is amidst us. *Being* is the art that shapes and molds our *daily identity*. We can only *be* when we *know* who we come from.

What is *daily identity*? It's a dose of alignment with our authentic God-given image. Learning how to be is learning how to dwell with God every day. Learning to live with God daily puts death to religion and life to relationship. Let's end the church theatrics and religious routines. Let's not act like attending church on Sunday is salvation or going to the soup kitchen counts as devotion. Where is your *heart*? Your heart, love, and service coincide to paint the picture of your identity. "For where your treasure is, there your heart will be also" (Matthew 6:21).

Identity Crisis

> *Do not love yourself based on your capabilities, work, or qualifications. Love yourself based on God's perception and His direction of love. If you do that, you will find your identity right where it began—in truth.*

What if I based my worth on my qualifications? I didn't go to college. Nobody has handed me a degree and said congratulations. My dream college since eighth grade was Columbia College Chicago. I had it all planned out; I'd live in downtown Chicago, study TV and Radio Broadcasting, and visit my family as often as I could. I even knew the nearest food spots. I remember the day I received my acceptance letter to Colombia; my dream had come true!

Then came the summer of 2017, and it was as if God was interrupting *all* my plans. To me, I just had a big loss because I told everyone I was going to my dream school; I was *accepted.* Then I felt God tugging on me, and suddenly, I felt like this was not my route at this time in my life. At this point, I had a YouTube channel, speaking on what I knew of purity and internal wellness. I felt God pulling me toward public speaking to some extent, but

I was consumed with the idea of not being *qualified*. I felt like I didn't have a capable bone in my body to go God's route. So, I tried my way again. I pursued a community college, but this time, my identity was stolen. I ran into an *actual* identity crisis. God sure does have a sense of humor. Societal pressure caused me to build my life, and the next thing I knew, *I didn't even exist*. Why? We aren't called to exist in spaces that were never in God's plan. We were created to operate from obedience, and my disobedience uncovered my identity. When we fight to be where God never called us, He'll recalibrate and remind us of who we are.

I began talking to God about my identity and where my identification would be acceptable to Him. I asked Him, "Where do I belong?" One day, it became clear, and I was realigned. It didn't come from my desire, family, or friends; *I heard God*. He led me to do what was impossible in my eyes. At seventeen, I pursued ministry and hosted conferences and events on *purity*. He gently nudged me to devote my life to serving others in this way. So, I said "Nope" again and found myself conflicted because I *heard* God but didn't obey. After a long journey of anxiety and fear, I finally obeyed, and here I am, years into being a certified, Holy Spirit-led *Humanity Shifter*. I get to share hope for a living. I am not certified in much anything else, but I do have a call on my life, and I was chosen by God.

So are you. ***You are a certified Humanity Shifter*-**at your job, in your community, in your family, and beyond. You have incredible impact.

In order to love what you do, you need a gift, and He has already given you this gift. I could list my accolades, my résumé, and my awards to prove something, but I'd much rather take pride in being led where I'm secure, devoted, and seen. Everything you need is already inside of you, but you must seek after the Father and unwrap it; you must obey. Purge for purity, be set apart, be obedient, take care of yourself, and do not base your worth on status or ranking. Do not make decisions based on the salary, the status, or the success. Make decisions based on obedience. I'm not suggesting not to attend college; I am suggesting obedience. God will not judge us according to our high-paying salary, knowledge, or the letters after our name. We will be judged based on our faithfulness and obedience to God. You have more to offer than qualities and positions. You are purposed for something, BUT your purpose is not your identity; it is your gifting. More than likely, though, your gift will enhance your love and appreciation for life. In many situations, the enemy will give you a reason why you "can't," why you "aren't," or who you should have been already. The enemy will even use the people you love to keep you from the Father and the gift He has given you. Sometimes, you are your greatest enemy, and if the enemy is powerless when God is in us, we just need more of Jesus Christ.

In order to secure your identity, *make* the enemy powerless over your life. Whenever you find yourself *doubting, blaming, or discrediting* yourself, you must know that you have the power through Christ to cancel every negative force. Start declaring truth over yourself. Second Corinthians 10:5 says, "We demolish arguments and every pretension that sets itself up against the knowledge of God, and we take captive every thought to make it obedient to Christ."

You are royalty; you were fashioned and woven by the finest Maker—God.

Do you have these thoughts?

"I failed when I made a promise."

"I regret what I did."

"I don't feel good enough for God."

"I haven't made progress."

If so, here is what you can say to misidentification:

I failed when I made a promise, but I have this moment to repent and change.

> Repent, then, and turn to God, so that your sins may be wiped out, that times of refreshing may come from the Lord. (Acts 3:19)

I know that condemnation is not from the Father, so I have an opportunity to cast my cares on Him and reset.

> If we confess our sins, he is faithful and just to forgive us our sins and to cleanse us from all unrighteousness. (1 John 1:9 ESV)

I'm not good enough for God, but He never told me to be good in my own strength; He called me to be faithful.

> No, in all these things we are more than conquerors through him who loved us. For I am convinced that neither death nor life, neither angels nor demons, neither the present nor the future, nor any powers, neither height nor depth, nor anything else in all creation, will be able to separate us from the love of God that is in Christ Jesus our Lord. (Romans 8:37–39)

I haven't made progress, but I can start now.

> "Even now," says the LORD, "Turn and come to Me with all your heart [in genuine repentance], With fasting and weeping and mourning [until every barrier is removed and the broken fellowship is restored]; Rip your heart to pieces [in sorrow and contrition] and not your garments." Now return [in repentance] to the LORD your God, For He is gracious and compassionate, Slow to anger, abounding in lovingkindness [faithful to His covenant with His people]; And He relents [His sentence of] evil [when His people genuinely repent]. (Joel 2:12–13 AMP)

Being a true lover of your soul means consistently looking for ways to improve day by day. True self-love is not stagnant or selfish; it is in constant pursuit of construction and progression for the well-being of the world *in* you. When you get to a certain level of inner love, you will find yourself wanting more than a horoscope, enneagram, fortune cookie, degree, or self-pleasure. The discovery is everlasting and cannot be measured or determined by a quote, trait, attribute, or feeling but is forever internalized in wonder, dissection, liberation, and truth. Lean into perfection (Jesus Christ) every day, and eventually, you will find yourself loving *you* more than ever. We all know that "nobody is perfect," but we should never use that as an excuse to stay complacent. Philippians

3:12 says, "Not that I have already obtained it [this goal of being Christlike] or have already been made perfect, but I actively press on so that I may take hold of that [perfection] for which Christ Jesus took hold of me and made me His own" (AMP).

Love is growth; love is a viewfinder, and love is a *mirror*. When you understand that the root of self-love is self-dissection, you will excel in your identity and, eventually, shift the world around you.

Postured Identity

What does royalty look like? If we truly embrace who we are, we will not question our value or have to prove it. Royalty is the state of finding rest in your humility and finding strength in submission. I don't mean submission in the slavery sense; I mean submission in the humbling sense. It takes a humble person to embrace their identity. When the world suggests a plan, yet you follow God's plan—this is humility. Thinking that you're better than any person on this earth because of what you look like, what you've done, or what you've earned keeps you from a life of true royalty. Be confident, but understand that your accomplishments only reflect what you have been *capable* of, not what you're *worthy* of.

If I had a thousand tongues, I could not tell you how flawed people are. People are very "people-y," and it's exhausting thinking about the fake, phony, copy-and-paste "Christians" who think it's okay to manipulate, gaslight, take advantage of kingdom matters, and on top of that, still serve in the church, be appointed, and have active leadership roles. This is not God's will for the church. Don't lose heart; for those of us who have been wounded by trusted people, there is an internal revival awaiting. Pain caused by a trusted source is not a call to curse our enemies; we're actually called to bless them, according to Luke 6:28. God will handle what we're too weak even to discuss.

We must be especially careful in leadership positions. We must not leap into responsibilities and titles that we have not been processed for yet. In the same way, we must not despise or reject where God has placed us in comparison to them. We do not need a megaphone when we are wounded, nor do we need social media when we're offended. Royalty means becoming low, peaceable, and humble. Your time will come, but likely not when you have an opportunity to tear your enemies down. Just because your spirit is excited does not mean that God is in agreement. Just because leaders are wrong doesn't make us right. God is the ultimate revealer of our hearts, and we will *all* be judged for what is in our hearts. Our identity can only go as far as our humility, and *nothing* will be left in the dark.

> For there is nothing covered that will not be revealed, nor hidden that will not be known. Therefore whatever you have spoken in the dark will be heard in the light, and what you have spoken in the ear in inner rooms will be proclaimed on the housetops. (Luke 12:2–3 NKJV)

Do not store up for yourselves treasures on earth, where moths and vermin destroy, and where thieves break in and steal. But store up for yourselves treasures in heaven, where moths and vermin do not destroy, and where thieves do not break in and steal. For where your treasure is, there your heart will be also. The eye is the lamp of the body. If your eyes are healthy, your whole body will be full of light. But if your eyes are unhealthy, your whole body will be full of darkness. If then the light within you is darkness, how great is that darkness! (Matthew 6:19–23)

The Royal Victim

Victimization is the narrative that ripples worldwide. A victim mentality is one that is full of lies, self-loathing, and a "woe is me" mentality. Playing the victim role makes it easy to manipulate, control, and deceive. I'm calling out *the royal victim*.

As someone who has been forced against my will, I do not claim the victim title because it produces a victim mentality. A rooted identity does not sulk and self-medicate via manipulation.

> *We become just as bad as the perpetrator when we produce manipulative ways to win others over with our pain.*

Self-pity only creates spaces for a hardened heart. You become a dark reflection when you take little to no responsibility for your actions or position. This is *false humility*. This mindset convinces us that we are never at fault and *they* just need to change *their* ways. However, when we become coachable, teachable, and correctable, we become childlike, and when we become childlike, we become children of God and truth.

I carried an orphan mentality for many years but I've learned that the orphan could become everything they wanted and everything they didn't even know they wanted to be yet.

This is the part where we are humbled in surrender. I became who I thought I could never become. Disobedience is not always turning your ear from God; it is also inclining our ear to ourselves, leaving little to no room for truth. I learned more from the person who assaulted me than I learned from anything else in life. The lesson I chose to receive after being assaulted was to forgive because the assaulter was also hurting. Have compassion because the other person is in a process as you are. Instead of adopting the narrative that I'm a victim of assault, I learned that the assaulter was assaulted. This led me to see that **we all need saving**. The orphan attempted to produce another orphan, but God had a plan. We love because we don't deserve the love we receive; love is undeserving yet willing. I'm not saying give people a pass for their wrongdoing, but I am championing you toward a heart of humility.

Contrary to popular belief, you are not a victim, and people are not always against you. Let your victim guard down and be free. Let go of the mentality that nobody understands you. You're understood by the most valuable entity in creation, and if that's not enough, there's surely nothing that people can say or do to validate your pain. God deals with the proud just as He rewards the humble. I simply want to remind you of who you are.

> You are not a product of that environment.
>
> You are not what happened to you.
>
> You are not what they said about you.
>
> You no longer have to prove yourself.
>
> You are not hated.
>
> You are more than your body.

You are not an orphan.

You are not held captive.

You are handcrafted, and what happened to you does not define you.

God is bigger than the blemishes. **Be free.**

Devotion

Our devotion will ultimately become the fruit we eat and the fragrance we carry. If you worship your ideas, you become them. If you obsess over your significant other, you may become what he or she wants you to be. If you value your friends' opinions more than God's leadership, you may become the opinions. If you have a goal that is more important than letting it go, you may have an idol. Your devotion is only as good as your obedience, and if you ignore God's voice, you forfeit your greatest expression. Being a part of the body of Christ means humbling yourself to the point of *total surrender*. What it costs *never* matters. If it's my whole life, my whole relationship, my whole friend group, my whole identity, my whole diet, my whole emotion, or my whole career—God take it.

This is what it's like to sit in the middle of royalty. You can walk into a room and think you're the most significant because you have the futuristic car with the spaceship doors, but let me tell you—it doesn't matter. Nobody cares except the people who want to benefit from your prosperity.

Your success only matters to the people who want to take advantage of calling you their friend for the sake of their credibility.

Your desires fulfilled have the opportunity to harm you in the wrong season versus bless you in the right one. The things that you possess are only an *addition* to what you hold in your heart, not a trophy. Be careful of what you praise or take comfort in; it will shape you.

When we are rejected, we do one of two things:

1. We hide in hopes that no one notices us.
2. We become extravagant in hopes that someone or everyone will notice us.

Become the person who neither hides nor becomes extravagant. Become the humble, truthful, honest person who delights in truth, life, edification, and authenticity. Masking the pain of rejection causes an orphan mentality, which damages the world around us.

Character

You have likely heard all your life that "actions speak louder than words." Taking inventory of the seemingly small things creates an incredibly impactful ripple effect. Notice how significant small things are to you. For example, a small gesture like someone holding the door for you after a long day or a kind gesture at your local market. It's time to develop good character for the sake of unity. This builds a muscle that blocks habitual dysfunction and assumption. Intentionality develops character because you begin to pay attention to small, intricate details. Whether you're a stranger, a friend, a sister, a brother, a co-worker, a mother, or a father, your character matters.

Your ability to change another person's life based on your actions is greater than you know.

Building character builds royalty and speaks volumes to your identity. If you want to be a person of valor, you never slander a name; you never bash or tear down another person. You must always strive to be the best you can be to others. We will not be perfect at this, but if we try, we will notice that love will be reciprocated—maybe not from that friend, family member, or co-worker, but we will surely be given in return the lost love from God. God sees the seeds. If He plants you in that location, your job is to water—become a deep, refreshing breath to those around you. Rid yourself of gossip, slander, cursing, and name-calling, and do not develop drama. Bring the peace, and be the peace. This develops your ability to steward people and interactions well. A royal response is a rooted identity.

Influence

Most people are not kings or queens or bosses; they are simply people with impact.

> *Impact is dangerous in the possession of ignorance and evil.*

Most people with impact are simply people with a strong influence. But what are they *doing* with the influence? We live in a time when twerking and bikinis are praised, and substance abuse and aggressive behavior are accepted. Even young children want to wear fewer and fewer clothes, and parents see no problem with it. As a society, we have normalized things and ways that should have never become normal. Royalty has become TikTok stars who worked toward fame and fortune rather than internal substance and joy.

My life's mission is to tear down what the enemy has attempted to build up. Influence is *not* identity. Why can't influence be your identity? Because if you lost it all today, who would you be? Who would you serve? Why do you live? You can gauge who and what has the most influence when you walk out your door in the morning. When you stub your toe, what word do you use? When someone cuts you off in traffic, what do you do? These seemingly small reactions contribute to the world around us and, eventually, have global impact. Influencers need to come to a place where their influence is bettering the one, the one hundred, and the one hundred million. Where impact and influence are given, most people abuse, and only a few rise to represent royalty well. You are not rejected, you are not less than, and you are not an embarrassment. You don't need to be noticed to be accepted. We don't have to strive for the things that will not sustain us. Rise up as a member of the royal priesthood that you are; you are expensive, bought with a price. "For ye are bought with a price: therefore glorify God in your body, and in your spirit, which are God's" (1 Corinthians 6:20 KJV).

Nothing compares to the detail of you.

Your identity is far from an accolade, pronoun, body type, personality, or lip plumper. Your identity is a deep well of contribution to a purpose far beyond you.

You matter more than you think because you contribute more than you know.

Season 3: Pink

The Depth of Love (Experiencing Authentic Love)

We were born into a bloodline of sovereignty—an elite class called love.

Identified Love

Maybe the level of love you give yourself is based on what you never did right. You got back into the relationship, you started drinking again, or you reconnected with the friends who gave attention but not wisdom. Maybe you feel toxic to others around you; you fall back into your past addictions, you begin to realize that you are human, and you fall. Maybe you made the excuse to stay on the ground, so you fell into a space of self-hatred and began unknowingly living a life full of lies. Now, you wallow in your sorrow because you never reached your own expectation of love. You failed yourself, so you think that God looks at you as "the one who failed."

We tend to subconsciously base love for self on a meter of perfection or a personality test. If I do this right, I love myself more, but if I do it wrong, my self-love disintegrates. I have to do it this way because I'm conforming to my horoscope, love language, enneagram, or who I would *rather* be. There then becomes a level of self-righteousness, where you'll never be wrong, which is also dangerous. Copying or wanting to be someone or something you aren't is not embracing your art, and it's offensive to the artist. *Do away with this faulty religious mindset.* Resisting wisdom or input is not embracing truth; it's pride.

Embracing your true identity is embracing authentic correction; this is love. If the people in your life only hype you up and stroke your ego, this is a problem. We all need people who will tell us, in love, when we are wrong or how we could have improved.

The way that you *respond* to correction reveals your heart. You should *never* always be right because that's impossible. There should be apology, consideration, deep reflection, and evaluation flowing out of you. The love that you have for yourself should be as patient—and as passionate—as the time you spend waiting for your lover to respond. We tend to be so patient in moments of eagerness, waiting in expectation of a response that will be less than a grain of what we *need*. We seem to tolerate improper care yet neglect goodness. We seem to wait as long as it takes to be seen by a lackluster love yet forget that true love has no lack and no expiration date. The best kind of love is a love that looks inward and takes time to ask, "Where am I wounded so that I can love well? Where am I bleeding so I can heal the wounds of self-hatred to be loved well?"

> Why do you look at the speck of sawdust in your brother's eye and pay no attention to the plank in your own eye? How can you say to your brother, "Let me take the speck out of your eye," when all the time there is a plank in your

own eye? You hypocrite, first take the plank out of your own eye, and then you will see clearly to remove the speck from your brother's eye. (Matthew 7:3–5)

> *We simply cannot love our neighbor if we don't first love ourselves, and we can only love ourselves if we know the source of love.*

It's not in our nature to desire God, but it is what we're made for. Mark 12:30–31 says, "'Love the Lord your God with all your heart and with all your soul and with all your mind and with all your strength.' The second is this: 'Love your neighbor as yourself.' There is no commandment greater than these."

There was a time when I perceived self-love as finding someone to validate love for me. I thought a relationship would magnify that love so that I wouldn't have to love myself. It did validate something—brokenness. I couldn't stand the idea of "healing" first.

> *Running away from (or rejecting) healing only confirmed that something within me needed to be healed.*

My way of avoiding healing was "falling in love" with someone who could love me deep enough to distract the love that needed to be found in Christ. This is when I began to idolize relationships. This is also when I found out that God plays no games, and He doesn't want His children to live lukewarm lifestyles. When we resist God, our spirit resists truth. Then, we wonder why chaos and darkness surround us. This revelation caused conviction. I made the approval of man greater than the affirmation of Christ. Now, I strive to subject the approval of man under my feet daily so that I can recognize love.

Here are a few things I did to seek the love that I needed and to focus on the Father:

Purge for purity. Get off social media for a minimum of one year, and watch how your mind will turn to new depth and wonder. You may be bored initially, but you will begin to discover you more than the item or trend on social media that you don't possess. Life and identity are not about hearts, shares, attention, or comments. There is no number—of friends, likes, or followers—higher than your life's value. If you find yourself posting to be agreed with or seen, purge for purity by removing yourself from any social situations that do not add value to your life.

Be original. If we didn't compare ourselves to others so much, we would probably still be wearing brands from 2001 (although even THAT'S a trend now). It is cool to be set apart and be different. Be a trendsetter, write a book, produce music, paint, or be a clown at a carnival! Do what brings you authentic JOY; do the thing that puts some pure-hearted pep in your step. Even if that thing doesn't produce capital, do it. God wants you to live fulfilled. Jumping on bandwagons produces temporary gratification but never internal impact. You have an original, authentic expression. Ask God what that looks like for you because He will reveal His will for your life if you ask Him. "Ask and it will be given to you" (Matthew 7:7).

> So we look not at the things which are seen, but at the things which are unseen; for the things which are visible are temporal [just brief and fleeting], but the things which are invisible are everlasting and imperishable. (2 Corinthians 4:18 AMP)

> Ask and keep on asking and it will be given to you; seek and keep on seeking and you will find; knock and keep on knocking and the door will be opened to you. For everyone who keeps on asking receives, and he who keeps on seeking finds, and to him who keeps on knocking, it will be opened. Or what man is there among you who, if

> his son asks for bread, will [instead] give him a stone? Or if he asks for a fish, will [instead] give him a snake? If you then, evil (sinful by nature) as you are, know how to give good and advantageous gifts to your children, how much more will your Father who is in heaven [perfect as He is] give what is good and advantageous to those who keep on asking Him. (Matthew 7:7–11 AMP)

There have been *countless* times in my life when I've asked God questions, and I never heard His answer. Just because we don't hear His voice every moment doesn't mean He didn't speak. Nevertheless, this is an exhausting place to be. Sometimes, when we don't hear God's voice, it's a call to rest in the information we have now because *now* is all we need today. There is love and grace even in seasons of uncertainty. Trust that your identity is being refined and revealed.

Your *why* always reveals your *who*, and your *who* always reveals your *why*. I love (why?) because (Who?) He first loved me. 1 John 4:19: "We love because he first loved us."

The Source of Love

Whose love do you represent? What is the source of your love? Have you found the positive energy from the universe that fills your heart with perfection? If you said yes, I believe you because God created the universe. The sun, the moon, and the stars are all by Him. God is the source, the wind in the winds, the heat in the night, He is the brisk in the cold. He is the King of all kings and Lord of all lords, and I'm not writing to convince you of this love; I'm writing to direct you to the depth and personality of His love. I just want to introduce you or reconnect you. If I've felt it, anyone can. If I've actually believed in a power that I cannot see, anyone can. I don't believe in my *Who* because I need inspiration to get through my day, although this is a part of the relationship. I believe in my Who because I need a reason to live. I need to know why I live and Who I live for so that in every moment, I have something to look forward to. It must be more than family. It must be more than friends, more than these gas prices, more than my cat, my dog, my possessions, and my addictions. When all things pass away, and it's just me against the world, *who* **am I**? Should I wallow because I can't live without the things I love? Or shall I rejoice because I know I am in God's hands?

Love calls for perseverance, but pain tends to numb the heart and cause friction between love's truth and lust's lie. Many of us become weary of loving because we simply don't know love. If we don't have a working knowledge of love, we can't know *how* to love. We mask love with what we call "self-love," which, in reality, has become self-service and selfish. Love has been minimized to appearance, maintenance, and the number of outings we go on per week. If we ask God what love truly is, I think He would identify it as the most selfless, inconvenient, thoughtful, and careful act. Love has nothing to do with your ability to work out three or four days per week because when you break that commitment, where exactly does the love *go*? To put love in perspective, we must see it *purely* for what it is.

> *Love is a selfless death.*

I remember a time when I was consumed with the idea of marriage because I couldn't wait to post the cutest photos of my relationship (ya know, #relationshipgoals). That time may have been yesterday, but that's not the point here. During this time, I was awakened to the truth that my idea of love was based on the approval and recognition of *people*. I valued marriage so that I could be *seen*, but what if God made marriage so that we would *die*? What do I mean? It's likely that our modern-day version of love is misconstrued because we want comfort. As an unmarried woman, I've learned in solely walking with Jesus that **love is compromise** and not always comfortable. Love is never microwaveable; love is cooked slow, on low. We become less so that love can arise and become more. I'm convinced that we're ready to be married once we're ready to be selfless. If my conclusion is true, some of us may never become "ready," but we'll have the grace to love well when it's time.

Dating

The blood that was shed on the cross and that flesh that was tearing at its inmost core is the greatest example that we've seen of love in *all* of history. This is why I have a *personal* conviction that the world's way of dating is not God's plan. I would be dishonest if I said that I have not been on dates. Furthermore, I'd be dishonest if I said I did not enjoy the dates thoroughly. There's absolutely nothing wrong with setting a date and time on a calendar with an individual that we may have an interest in, but before we do, we must understand that love is not temporal; it's everlasting. Love does not question longevity; love either *is* or is not. Love was designed to *unify and last*. Dating around the way culture does splits God's intended design for love and marriage into "build-a-spouse." When it doesn't happen *our* way, we become discouraged and question if love is for us. It's my conviction that God will lead us to our spouse and speak clearly when the time is right.

> *I believe we end up heartbroken, confused, and, sometimes, even bitter when we manipulate the sovereignty of God and call it free will.*

Culture enters into temporary relationships that were never intended to expire. I've dated around in the past and only ended up with lessons, yet no love.

Am I suggesting that it's wise to marry without knowledge of someone? No. Am I suggesting or *persuading* you not to date? No. Am I suggesting that you be spirit-led and sober-minded according to the Word? Yes. Sure, God can "use" anything, but I believe we have manipulated freedom and used it as an excuse for God's grace to run with our desire—even I'm guilty of this. **God's grace is not God's approval.** I believe our ignorance is covered by God's mercy. I believe our mistakes are covered by God's grace. Let's not take this for granted.

> *Love is perfect; it is not intended nor created to expire.*

Granted, there's no perfect human on this earth, but we should recognize the traits of love to recognize how to *be* loved, how to love *well*, and how to *accept* love. I don't desire to do what culture does because culture stays relevant, but culture doesn't lead us to love and longevity. Following cultural routines and suggestions can lead to heartbreak and keep us from real love. I suggest that if dating, we get to know the human, not the hormones, and when choosing, we understand love, not lust. We can determine the difference when we know the character of God, which is, ultimately, His love.

Heartbreak

Whether we do life biblically, aligning our lives with God the best we can, or we come up short and mess up, we can still stumble upon this thing called heartbreak. It's gut-wrenching, life-changing, and hurtful. When pursuing love, you might get a response you didn't want or weren't expecting from the person you desire to be with. It seems as though the deeper we go with God, the more distractions arise. The enemy wants to keep us the furthest he can from knowing love, so he will attempt to trap us in heartbreak. Maybe that crush didn't like you back, or as soon as you and your spouse finally go to church together, there's opposition. There's a reason for this in the enemy's camp, but there's a purpose for this in God's kingdom.

Disappointment is an opportunity for depth.

Rejection is an opportunity to persevere. It's all about how we respond and what we embody in the face of opposition. It's okay to be hurt, and it's normal to cry when wounded, but God wants to see your knee-jerk reaction to offense and heartbreak.

"Bear with each other and forgive one another if any of you has a grievance against someone. Forgive as the Lord forgave you" (Colossians 3:13). When you're offended by either what God or man says, you should take into account the decision that will be produced *after* the offense. The enemy attempts to use offense as an object to blind you to love.

> *When your heart is bitter, you cannot recollect goodness.*

When bitter, you can't taste with a cleansed palate or see with clear eyes. This is why before pursuing love, *dissecting, asking, and developing* are crucial. With these three steps, we're training our first response to be in love (clarity, purity, and truth) to prevent the result of heartbreak. Let's tear down the fear of rejection due to our past to prevent future bitterness and pain. This is applicable to any loss or internal trauma that still needs to be forgiven or settled.

Navigating Heartbreak

Step 1: Dissect

Take time to dissect the past or current situation by looking at what I like to call "notice points." It may hurt, but taking action steps to heal from heartbreak will result in a sober mind and deeper love.

Take intentional time to reflect and respond:

Was/am I mad at the other person or mad at me? Who am I placing blame on? Am I disappointed in myself, God, or someone else?

Where have I stored anger, and how is it presenting itself? Is it in my mind, body, soul, or spirit? How do I react to opposition?

What do/did you notice beyond appearance? Looks can be deceiving, so look beyond what meets the eye. What is the person's intention? Were you blinded by what you decided to hear or see?

What do/did you notice beyond character? Sometimes, the initial character you see can be distorted. Depending on the day, time, or season, it seems we can all have clouded judgment. Examine the true character of the person. This takes time and patience!

What do/did you notice beyond words? Don't have itching ears; be vigilant, even if someone says all the right things. See someone rightly and clearly; do not put words in his mouth or take something out that she did not say.

People can look, act, and say anything they want, but it's not until you begin to *dissect* the intention, heart, and motive of the person that you discover who that person truly is. It might take time, but often, discernment will help you to dissect. Then, once you dissect, you can begin to communicate effectively rather than taking offense.

What action will you take to start dissecting?

_____

_____

_____

_____

_____

_____

Step 2: Ask

Next, how do you discern? Ask God these questions:

What posture do I take? Do I respond sternly, quietly, or

suggestively? Is my response internal or literal?

How do I forgive someone? What can I do to release that person from my heart and mind?

What does obedience look like for me? Do I put it on the shelf and give it time, or does it need to be addressed/released right away?

What do you need to ask God? What will you do based on what He says?

_____

_____

_____

_____

_____

_____

Step 3: Develop

Now, you develop:

1. A mental, tangible *strategy* for remaining at peace
2. A solidified *plan* of how you will persist in love

3. A working *relationship* with God, regardless of the outcome or their actions

Love is, at times, offensive. Love is the ability to hear something unpleasant and then await the heart and intention of whoever that information is coming from, even God. Once we have a response from God, we have the opportunity to begin to live in greater correction and submission, even if we don't agree with the answer. There is no love if there is no correction. Love is on a spectrum that we believe is birthed from rainbows, butterflies, and chocolates on Valentine's Day. What I have now come to understand is that love can be pain—and yes, no pain, no gain. Love is a patient, sacrificial action.

Here are the ways to identify love in its simplicity.

> Love is patient and kind; love does not envy or boast; it is not arrogant or rude. It does not insist on its own way; it is not irritable or resentful; it does not rejoice at wrongdoing, but rejoices with the truth. Love bears all things, believes all things, hopes all things, endures all things. Love never ends. As for prophecies, they will pass away; as for tongues, they will cease; as for knowledge, it will pass away. (1 Corinthians 13:4–8 ESV)

Reflect on this:

Do you love well?

How do you love?

How do you respond to love?

Where do you lack love?

How can you embody love?

_____

_____

_____

_____

_____

_____

> If we reject discovering new ways to love *well*, we reject Christ's call to love. We should constantly be living in consideration of how to love better. The consideration of love produces a pure heart. "Blessed are the pure in heart: for they shall see God" (Matthew 5:8 KJV).

The Absence of Love and Its Rejection

When my dad left for years on end to do whatever he went to do that was seemingly more important than his four children and his wife, I was deeply wounded by his absence. I called often and became accustomed to the automated voicemail: "Your call has been forwarded to an automated voice message system. The person you're trying to reach is not available. At the tone, please record your message."

Even worse, "This person's mailbox is full." *Beep, beep, beep.*

Staring at my phone's home screen reminded me of rejection from my father; it seemed like he didn't want to talk to me. "*Where was he? What could be more important?*" I thought.

As a daughter, I searched for my father's love and couldn't always find it.

Love is a Dance

I vividly remember wanting to go to the fourth-grade Daddy Daughter Dance. It was in disappointment of my father's absence, yet gratitude, that I reached out and asked my uncle to take me in place of my father. Of course, my uncle had no hesitation, yet my heart became even more broken. As a nine-year-old girl just wanting to show up with her dad, I felt rejected by the one I loved because I needed an alternative.

My dad kept me guessing if he would be present or not, and I wondered . . . I waited . . . and I wondered more. Until one day, I got a box in the mail. In this box was an extra-large black bag; it smelled *just* like my dad! The smell of his essential oils filled the room as I scrambled to open this mystery. In that bag was the most beautiful white ball gown. Since my dad was miles and miles away, he had mailed me a dress for the dance! Not *only* a beautiful white gown but accessories and my first heels. I was anxious to try it on, and it fit—my dad knew my size! My heart was somewhere between joy and having a lot of questions. With somewhat of a hole in my heart, I made up my mind that would be the dress I would wear to the dance with my uncle. I genuinely didn't know if my dad would show up. The big day finally came, and . . . he showed up! A little late, according to my schedule, but *he showed up*. You'd think I'd be jumping for joy, but truthfully, *I was hurt*. The one I trusted left me guessing about his presence. At this point, it didn't matter much that he showed up because I had to prepare without him.

SHIFT HUMANITY

Correction and submission are better received when there's an active and loving relationship, but wounds make love difficult to receive.

When you're wounded, you begin to reject love due to your history with it. I always thought love would be delayed and show up halfway. Even if our experience of love shows up halfway, we must heal from expectation. We tend to decipher love based on one or a few occurrences, but those occurrences were an attempt to *hinder* love, not develop it. Although it wasn't according to my plan, my dad loved me in his way on his terms. There was space between us, but the desire for healing let me receive my dad right where and when he met me. Love is choosing to accept the best part of a person, not crucify the worst of them. That night, I realized that love doesn't always show up in ways that we develop in our minds and will.

> *We must yield ourselves to the possibility that love is something other than what we have experienced or expected.*

Culturally, most would develop a trace of bitterness and hostility toward the lack of love, but I've seen that, through Christ, there's a love that abounds the flesh and shell of a person. Although my dad wasn't as present as I would've liked him to be, I know he thought of me. I'm not suggesting that you accept lackadaisical love; I'm encouraging you to recognize how loved you are rather than accept the love you lacked. When it comes to God, we may not feel Him, see Him, or even experience His love, but His love can come in the form of preparation. His love can come in the form of His thoughts about us. His love can come as His comforting presence when waiting seems impossible to endure. His love can come as Him showing up although you had alternative plans. My point is that God shows up *every* time. My dad was human, and we must separate human love from God's love.

That person who let us down is human, and we must not be wounded by the scars of man or woman but rather healed by the scars of Christ.

That trusted friend who abused us is human, and we must not be wounded by the scars of man or woman but rather healed by the scars of Christ.

The God that promised you love is a sovereign, true, *good* God, and we must not be wounded by the scars of man or woman but rather healed by the scars of Christ.

Once we can remove the wounds of people from our hearts, we can see and experience God's love in a pure, refreshing way. Like a bride awaiting her groom, **love is coming**. Just like my dad's unexpected gift in the mail with my size, my own bow, and heels, God is sending you a package with your name on it. God's love is personalized for you. He's about to knock on the door of your heart; it's time to let go of what hindered love.

> Behold, I stand at the door and knock. If anyone hears My voice and opens the door, I will come in to him and dine with him, and he with Me. (Revelation 3:20 NKJV)

> Every good gift and every perfect gift is from above, coming down from the Father of lights, with whom there is no variation or shadow due to change. (James 1:17 ESV)

I want you to think about what has hindered love in your life. It could have been an ex, a friend, a spouse, a family member, a trusted colleague, or your own idea of how you perceive love. Identify that person, place, or thing. How did it cloud the truth about who God is?

_____

_____

_____

_____

_____

Despite his shortcomings, I know my father loved me. Even though he kept me guessing at times, he made his love known. I smelled the aroma of love in his cooking and heard his love in every sizzle until he called us down to eat. He always blasted Anita Baker, who is now my all-time favorite artist. We made our own dance to

"You're My Everything." We had so many inside jokes. When he was there, I can't remember a day when he didn't rub my chin and say, "My baby and her pointy chin; look at those almond eyes." My memories with him are full of love. Even though he's gone now, our love was never lost. The continuation of his love is just a mystery; I'll never know what it could have been. I sit in wonder of what he would have been like today. His love truly lasted until the day he left this life. I miss his love, but it never leaves. As I type, I laugh and cry in remembrance of how my father loved me oh so much, and I always hold onto that truth. I receive that truth. I was and am his baby girl. Oh, what I'd pay to dance with my father again.

Faithful Love

What is the posture humanity is called to take in loving God rightly? First, we should know how to be faithful. Experience with Christ does not equate to works; it equates to faithfulness. Do you keep your word? Do you follow through with your promises? Do you compromise because you have a sudden temptation? Do you boldly proclaim your salvation, or do you hide when God's name is mentioned?

We must evaluate our interests and ask ourselves who and what responses we are yielding to. How do you value yourself and others? How does love cause you to grow despite hardship? How does love thrust you into perseverance? You know you're ready to love when you're resilient. Resilience allows us to tap into an unstoppable grace to love called perseverance. Perseverance is equivalent to being faithful. Despite delay or doubt, you remain consistent in love in the face of opposition. You don't mind the upward climb as long as you're operating in love. Do not expect to receive any more than you give. *Love* is the ability to passionately pursue perseverance. You don't blindly accept everything that seems good, nor do you deny everything that feels negative. Taking steps into perseverance produces healthy relational love.

Loving Radically Beyond Trauma

Grace, mercy, redemption, and forgiveness empower us to love regardless of the other party's actions. There was a time when I loved hard just because receiving love was challenging. I could love you to death even if you despised me because I refused to let rejection get a grip on me again. Love can be easily given and should be contemplatively received according to the intentions of the one giving it.

> *When we love from a wounded place, we yearn for validation.*

Broken love comes from a place of longing, not offering. This is called false humility. We shouldn't love out of lack; *we should love by choice.* Inauthentic love is hesitant, and authentic love is actionable. What hinders love tends to break the heart, and what feeds love builds the soul and spirit.

We're All Human

Letting offense or lust get in the way of loving someone well is the way to bitterness; it will always end in heartbreak. Be certain that they love Christ before they choose to love you so that they may love you as Christ intended. Be certain that you love Christ above them so that *you* may love as Christ intended. Your relationships should look like nothing less than a passionate pursuit of Jesus because He is the standard. Love is then put into action through communication, change, and effort. In romantic relationships, friendships, or family, you should feel empowered to be better, do better, and live better because of who you give access to your life and vulnerability. The love of Jesus Christ shows us what He looks like daily through vibrant colors, people, music, sounds, and experiences. There are different shades of everything, whether light or dark. He reveals Himself in waves, winds, trees, plants, emotions, and feelings. He is here now, in your reading. The nearness of God is love, the passion of God is love, the essence of God is love, and whatever may have hindered love, may it all be replaced with true love. Stop accepting the false image or faulty sense of love that is common today. Instead, embrace the love that naturally rejects toxic behavior, embraces healthy conversation, cares to restore your tears to joy, avoids manipulation, and is an arc of safety.

If you let go of your belief of what *was* and look into the eyes of your heart to see the preparation of a new season, there may be blank pages. The beauty is that there are waves of revelation and relationship flowing to you today. The Comforter is here, always pursuing you. No matter what, lean into this love. It's time for love, and I'm talking about the consistent, lasting, and attentive kind of love—the one true living God kind of love.

Make this your prayer today: Heavenly Father, be the God of my heart when I need a home. Be the home in my heart when I need a God. Yahweh, reveal the truth to me. Let my life be proof of Your love, and let Your light be the reason why. Tend to the garden of my soul, in Jesus' name, Amen.

A Poem on Love

Light pink, hot pink, no in-betweens
Love is clear, love is consistent
Love pursues us, but so does lust
Love we must discern
Love is the pursuit of one's soul
Love is after your heart, not only the capsule that houses
your skin and bones
Love chastens
Love protects
Love gives
Love provides and creates; it's never selfish or lackluster
Love is passion
Love is a plea, asking for your hand to make you free
Free from hurt, free from pain, free from the lies that
were ordained
There's something about this love so passionate and pure
Agape, the love that will endure

My passion for this love is not in pursuit of a prize but His purpose, not a wedding but His will. Even if pleasure never finds its place in me, I will be satisfied with this love. Its pursuit is passionate. Its person is immaculate; His name is good. Love means embracing something we were given even when we question its validity. It's something all of us want, but none of us *fully* know.

Real Love

What if love disguises itself, and I fall into lust? We know the difference when we know the Father. He shares His love and never refrains. His is agape—the purest form of love. God's love provides clarity. There is one love who is embodied in three ways: the Father (God), the Son (Jesus Christ), and the Holy Spirit (our Guide). You don't have to prove something that already exists. That's like standing in front of an audience and telling them I'm at home when I'm clearly standing right in front of them. The evidence is right there. My existence is proof of love; therefore, I can just *be*. It tells me I am loved enough to be held emotionally, physically, and spiritually. The truth is proof that I am living; my *proof* is the truth that I am alive in this skin. I could sit here and list all the ways God loves His children. But I'll only give you one. He loves you enough to lead you. You don't have to fight for His love; you just have to look for it—seek and find. He has won; you may have just missed the call to accept the winning trophy due to a distorted worldview of lust and distractions. Love is consistently sitting there waiting for you. Love led you even when *you* forgot or when you disobeyed. To love is to inherit. Beauty for ashes, love in place of loss, joy above happiness, promises over wishes, longevity over temporary. He is leading us to inherit these things daily.

Receiving this love is beyond our ability to look up and see it. Receiving this love is far above the action; receiving this love is in the *response*. What is your response? Maybe you feel like you aren't good enough for this love. Maybe you don't think you meet the "requirements" to be radically loved by God. Maybe you fear not having control; you fear receiving another father's love because your own left you or never gave enough of himself. There are no prerequisites for God's love because perfect love knew you *first*.

> *There are no qualifications to meet the God who loved you first. Knowing God requires work; being known requires belief.*

Love does not manipulate; it is not sneaky. You do not have to question this love.

Maybe you grew up religious and not in a relationship with this love. I'm talking about a one-of-a-kind love that will never leave you or forsake you. Lust crawls; love carries. Discern the difference. Just because you don't receive love well does not mean you can't be loved by the One who *first* loved you. Just because you are ignorant of love does not mean you are exempt from *being* loved. You can learn to love and how to be loved, but if you want the real thing, you can only learn love from the giver of life—GOD, the Father. *When you have felt it, you can't ignore it.* It's like a pink highlighter—bright, captivating, and bold.

The Red Flag of Lust

Lust is typically experienced and seen as a strategy for relief, but it only leads to a lifestyle of striving. We were not created for lust but rather for *love*. Lust can show up in many ways, but mostly through subtle, gentle, and patient ways, deceiving you into believing that lust is love.

Here's how lust can present itself:

- You: insecure (a personal lack that calls for consistent alignment in Christ)
- On the other side of insecurity: the spirit of lust (never satisfied, tempting, chasing a "never-ending")

The spirit of lust is not only sexual. As a matter of fact, lust comes in many forms. A few include:

- Desperate for success: money, rank, status, relationships

- Sexual arousal/sexual fantasy: pornography, masturbation, questioning sexuality, passion
- Appearance (Proverbs 6:25): pride, arrogance, acceptance, approval, lusting after the approval of man

Lust comes from a source that never wants you to give up in the pursuit of it. It is constant, and it likes to fish for whoever will take the bait. It is *never* safe and *never* righteous, yet it is more than possible to overcome with the solution of yielding and reliance.

Season 4: Red

A Yielded Life (The Urgency in Yielding)

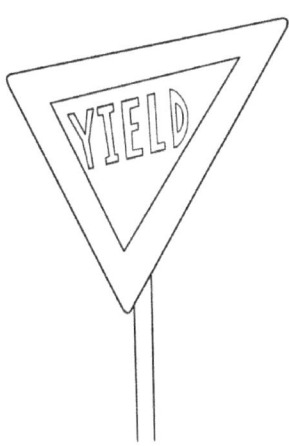

When approaching a yield sign, we must start to stop. You take your foot off the accelerator and begin to brake.

> *There's always a starting point to stopping defeat, and it begins with yielding to the Perfecter of our faith.*

It was middle school, and I had a feeling my dad wouldn't be around much longer after I watched a tear stream down his face, but not just any tear—a tear of blood. There was blood rushing from his eyes and nose. "Daddy, you're crying blood!" I said as he proceeded to ask me for a tissue. I was thirteen years old, not ever wanting to see my father again. Resistant and disgusted, I got his tissue. He never told me to cover my eyes or leave the room. He let me watch his doom, and it became too much for his princess to look at. Most nights, I couldn't sleep but lay with my eyes open, trembling in fear of my dying father just steps away from me. It became so bad to the point where he reeked of a foul body odor, and I tried to avoid him when I was home. He kept the door closed, and when it was opened, I held my breath walking past. The smell of death was in my nostrils, but this death journey didn't make me love him any less. I loved my dad. I didn't want to avoid him; I HAD to for my own mental health and wellness. I grew in disdain for being at home because it felt disgusting and dirty, and I felt trapped in a four-bedroom, three-bathroom suburban home. Home felt like death crying out. I was upset, angry, disgusted, and, most of all, tired of this. I was a hopeless girl needing saving.

On August 10, 2019, nearly six years after my dad's passing, I went downstairs to the bathroom. While I was in there, I looked at the floor and had a graphic flashback image of my dad lying on the bathroom floor with blood all over the light brown wooden panels. When I looked at that floor, I was reminded of the blood. It was now just a memory; it was gone and washed clean. God had transformed that bathroom from death to life. I never imagined that I'd use that bathroom again, but get this—the office that was his bedroom became mine. With a bright turquoise desk, shelves, my books, my mug collection, my storage, my rugs, my home studio. It was *my* space.

A *new* blood was shed.

In all suffering and strength, the blood was shed, and it washed me clean; my memories, doubts, and fears were washed away. This is redemption. For most of my teenage life, I'd carried the fear of the room that belonged to my dying father—now the room belongs to me. The keys of death are now access to light. I never thought that I'd understand why my daddy had to go, but because of the blood of Jesus, I see crystal clear what I once saw as death and doom. The shades would stay open, and I'd let the light shine in daily. There was constant, peaceful music playing from the radio that my mom left plugged in. The place where I was once most afraid became the same place where I have filmed some of my most heartfelt content. It became a place of life.

> *What was assigned to destroy you has the ability to catapult you.*

The blood of Jesus has plans of victory, prosperity, and life for you. That's why Jesus came—to demonstrate the love of God, our Father. Dad's blood helped remind me of the blood of Jesus Christ. Jesus hung on a cross, He was wounded for our transgressions, bruised for our iniquities, He suffered for us, and He died in our place. But then . . . He ROSE. Do you see the **red**emption power? Jesus went from death to life. He carried the weight of sin and death, and three days later, He rose out of the grave and ascended into heaven with all power and abundant life, now extending salvation. Thinking of my middle school soul watching my dying father puts me in remembrance of the beating, the scars, the taunting, and the pain of Christ. My tears today show me that the only way my soul awakened was because Jesus shed His blood so that I may live redeemed and free from every scar, image, and traumatic experience.

> *Healing begins when we put an end to the trauma that tried to kill us.*

That trauma is a wound that is only healed by the blood of Jesus. There's nothing that God cannot save. He is the God of redemption. He is perfect at rewriting stories, and He wants to get into the details of yours. Live in wonder of His love. You may not know it yet; you may not get it now, but you can have a friend on your way there. My soul went from death to life, my father went from life to death, and I now rejoice in knowing that it was, is, and will forever be nothing but the blood of Jesus that redeems. It's the perfect time to stop accepting defeat by letting go of self-pity and leaning into the victory that was given through the blood of Jesus Christ. He's capable of healing bodies, and He's more than able to heal trauma too. Let God evaluate your history and redeem your story; yield to His hand.

Overcoming Perfectionism

I recall my first in-studio radio interview. Anxiety was high. The first thing I told my mom when it was over was, "I think I did horrible, but there were a few things that I liked." Mind you, the interview was only scheduled to be ten minutes and turned out to be forty because the hosts loved the material so much that they kept extending my time on air. I was asked to pray over the listeners at the end, and I was also asked to come back. Many would equate my critique to perfectionism (and maybe it was), but I equate it to the pursuit of progression.

I am rarely 100 percent pleased with how things turn out, not because I wanted it to be perfect, but because I knew that it could be better if I'd just been more confident or showed up as my most authentic self. I knew what I would have been capable of if I didn't *allow* anxiety to creep in and if I pursued God more than pondered on the outcome. I wonder how prepared we would be if we spent intentional time on what was important. Perfectionism is a tactic from the enemy looking to taint your security in Christ more than it is your attempt to be perfect.

> *Perfectionism is not present without anxiety.*

Many of us strive for something that God does not intend for us in our current season, so we toil trying to figure out if He has a different plan. Pursuing an idea that's contrary to God's plan is anxiety-inducing. Philippians 4:6–7 says, "Do not be anxious about anything, but in every situation, by prayer and petition, with thanksgiving, present your requests to God. And the peace of God, which transcends all understanding, will guard your hearts and your minds in Christ Jesus."

Yielding to Deliverance

Deliverance is "a setting free; rescue or release." Deliverance is a process that you should look forward to. Why? Because there is freedom in deliverance. The most beautiful thing is being free from something that has held you back consciously or subconsciously for too long. Maybe that thing was an addiction, a feeling, a breakup, mental images of the past, or hurt from abuse; it could have been anything, and for all these years, you have fought the idea of becoming free and tamed by something called healing. The deliverance process *begins* when you invite Jesus to heal your heart *entirely*; it's called *yielding*. You lay down your desires and trade them all for His. He cares about the big, small, lowly, and tall. The journey won't always make sense, especially in the beginning, so I encourage you to pray the prayer below every day and act accordingly until you see a personal shift. "The righteous cry out, and the LORD hears them; he delivers them from all their troubles" (Psalm 34:17).

Lord, I am here as Your child, needing a healed heart. I ask that Your Holy Spirit give me the strength to live fully in what Your son Jesus died for. I invite You to consume my situations, invade my space, and take over my world. I ask that You rid me of my seemingly uncontrollable life and shape my heart to be postured to You alone. God, I desire You and Your will for my life. Deliver me from anything that is unlike You or takes up space where You reside, no matter what it takes, and carry me by Your grace, in Jesus' name, Amen.

If deliverance is also a formal or authoritative utterance, doesn't that mean that *we*, through the Spirit, have some form of power? Yes. Proverbs 18:21 says, "Death and life are in the power of the tongue: and they that love it shall eat the fruit thereof" (KJV).

In the deliverance process, the only way that you will conquer is if you allow yourself to. God is absolutely present, but He does not do the work *for* you. We must partner with Him to experience what He promised to happen in our lives. He stands with you as a *guide* with all power, but *your* desires must yield to *His* will.

> *There is always reality behind a dream, but dreams do not come true without effort.*

You must make intentional moves, fearless moves, *faith* moves. What does an intentional, fearless, faith move look like in the deliverance process? Going out of *your* way to conquer the same things that brought you *to* the deliverance process. As hard as this may be due to this thing called passion and desire, it's possible. Yielding to the Father calls us to submission so that we will not find ourselves lost in the process of healing with no direction. This is truly what dreams are made of.

Yielding in Passion

> I appeal to you therefore, brothers, by the mercies of God, to present your bodies as a living sacrifice, holy and acceptable to God, which is your spiritual worship. Do not be conformed to this world, but be transformed by the renewal of your mind, that by testing you may discern what is the will of God, what is good and acceptable and perfect. (Romans 12:1–2 ESV)

You must know that there will be moments or days when you have impure thoughts and human desires. Notice the Scripture says, "By TESTING you may discern what is the will of God," meaning: YOU WILL BE TESTED. Your desire to become healed may be flaming hot, but you can still be tempted. Being tempted or tested does not exempt you from the love of Christ, but this is a call to draw near to Him so that you will seek the Father who holds and protects your heart. When passion arises, you will feel your heartbeat and your body tingling in conviction. As soon as you know that something should not happen—flee! You must use the fruit of the Spirit (Galatians 5:22–23). While on my purity journey, I stumbled while I was hosting conferences, speaking at events, and encouraging others. I was still tempted to watch pornography while claiming devotion to living a purified lifestyle. This relapse was not a secret; it was a story that I was not willing to sweep under the rug to *appear* to be a better leader. In the world, this could either be a normal slip-up that is easily forgiven or a completely unforgivable sin that should put me in the pit. Yet, in the world of someone who truly desired to serve God free of bondage (me), I felt like I took so many steps in the wrong direction with a heart to want to do right. I began to actively sin on a regular, comfortable basis. Even in this, the passion of Christ never shamed me, and He kept no record of my wrongdoing. This is mercy. As *Humanity Shifters*, we are called to be unashamed. Not only unashamed in our faith but unashamed of our story. I knew that God was brewing a testimony in me as He is also in you.

Oftentimes, our life experiences become the very reasons why we need reliance on God.

What lifts us out of condemnation and into conviction is knowing that God knows you are human, but He also knows what you are capable of *because* of the cross. When we know better, we are called to do better. When I felt like I was going to, or even did, fall, or when I could have yielded but didn't, here is what God whispered in my weaknesses: "My flesh and heart may fail, but God is the strength of my heart and my portion forever" (Psalm 73:26).

Remember this: Purity=Progression, NOT perfection. Purity is the pursuit OF perfection, who is Jesus Christ.

- The Lord redeems.
- Repentance is key. Ask God for forgiveness. He forgives you easier than you forgive yourself.
- Forgive yourself.
- Find hobbies. Commit to reading the Bible. Pray. Seek.

> "But I say, walk by the Spirit, and you will not gratify the desires of the flesh" (Galatians 5:16 ESV).

Not only do we have control over what we allow ourselves to do, we can *choose* to control it. Some things are meant to be done in the realm that we have not yet seen. It's not about the porn; it's about the healing. Satan is never worried about what we do as long as he can *keep* us doing it. God has already fought for you, but it seems like passion and sin are on the defense. Sin is not only murder or cheating; it is anything that takes your attention off of the Father. God offers Himself *even* in our apprehension. Passion will present itself regardless, but yielding is in the decision and the conscious choice to pursue God.

Imagine driving, and you approach a yield sign. There is a car coming with the right of way; the lawful (and courteous) thing to do is to let the car with the right of way proceed. Yes, accidents happen, but signs are there to help prevent accidents. Be a child of God who yields and pays attention to the signs. Everything that you do impacts someone else. You never know how your sin may affect someone else's life. It's never just about you. Allow the Holy Spirit to go first, and then you follow along. The key to living a life that acknowledges God is to have a sin-conscious life—a lifestyle that trembles at God's underserving grace with a holy reverence.

Here are a few Scriptures to dwell on to stay clear of red flags:

> Therefore, since we have these promises, dear friends, let us purify ourselves from everything that contaminates body and spirit, perfecting holiness out of reverence for God. (2 Corinthians 7:1)

> But the Law came to increase and expand [the awareness of] the trespass [by defining and unmasking sin]. But where sin increased, [God's remarkable, gracious gift of] grace [His unmerited favor] has surpassed it and increased all the more, so that, as sin reigned in death, so also grace would reign through righteousness which brings eternal life through Jesus Christ our Lord. (Romans 5:20–21 AMP)

> So any person who knows what is right to do but does not do it, to him it is sin. (James 4:17 AMP)

> Now the practices of the sinful nature are clearly evident: they are sexual immorality, impurity, sensuality (total irresponsibility, lack of self-control), idolatry, sorcery, hostility, strife, jealousy, fits of anger, disputes, dissensions, factions [that promote heresies], envy, drunkenness, riotous behavior, and other things like these. I warn

> you beforehand, just as I did previously, that those who practice such things will not inherit the kingdom of God. (Galatians 5:19–21 AMP)

> For our struggle is not against flesh and blood [contending only with physical opponents], but against the rulers, against the powers, against the world forces of this [present] darkness, against the spiritual forces of wickedness in the heavenly (supernatural) places. (Ephesians 6:12 AMP)

When passion feels physical, know that there is something under that layer. This is a spiritual battle, not against your body, but against the blood. The flesh is the cavity; the soul is within. The soul is not what we see but what we feel. The soul does things that the flesh is incapable of doing. The flesh is an expression of the soul. This is why our choices matter. This is why when we feel tempted, we must flee by way of spiritual stamina because the attack is not only against your body; it is against your soul and spirit. We cannot compromise because we can't afford to!

Your purpose is greater than your pleasure and pain.

You are needed for the kingdom, and healing is necessary. Not everything that looks good *is good*. Let reality sink in, and seek the Lord with your *whole* heart.

Consider yielding for your own good and for the good of those who love the Lord.

You have a place here. You are not an accident. Your sins are forgiven. Maybe God is just waiting on you to forgive yourself and return to Him.

What If We Died?

What if, more times than not, we decided to ask ourselves what would happen if we were less of self and more of Him? What if we died to our passion and surrendered to His will and watched Him still fill us with the fragrance of sweet roses?

> *Who are we depriving of hope if we remain alive to our flesh?*

The blood was spilled to depict and *be* the pain that only He could endure for the evolution and elevation of mankind, not only for the prosperity of humanity but for the glorification of the Father. The blood was spilled so that we would not have to carry the burden of others or of self. He was nailed to a cross that we would never be able to stand, "like a rose trampled on the ground," as the beautiful song says. It took a perfect man to die to save generations upon generations, decades upon decades, and it was by nothing but the blood of Jesus. Now, we have a standard, a mandate, a duty, and one purpose: to glorify the worthy One who gives and takes away. With fear and trembling, may we bow.

Our Way or His Will

Society has abused what some call "free will." Assuming that we do have a choice in the way that we live, free will is not permission to sin. Free will *should* be yielded freedom. Free will is not an excuse to sin but also not an exemption from sinful nature and passionate, tempting scenarios. In my eyes, free will is simply flesh in motion. If it's not God's will, there's no way.

> Let no one say when he is tempted, "I am being tempted by God," for God cannot be tempted with evil, and he himself tempts no one. But each person is tempted when he is lured and enticed **by his own desire.** Then desire when it has conceived gives birth to sin, and sin when it is fully grown brings forth death. Do not be deceived, my beloved brothers. (James 1:13–16 ESV, emphasis mine)

Acceleration: Endurance and Discipline

God has "chosen ones" called the remnant. The remnant are the ones who will do whatever it takes until the end of time to serve God with their entire being. We are called and mandated to represent His standard of love and do it *quickly*. There is simply no time to drag our feet when the Savior of the world is coming soon. Now is the time to GO, GO, GO. With that creative gifting that He gave you, with the passion that you have in your field, with your character and integrity, with that pure heart you desire. GO. **He disciplines us in order to correct us, but correction does not equate to a lack of love.** You are not disqualified; you're simply being *disciplined*. God is the safety net that may feel unstable to our human experience. When you're *not* living in His will, there is no spiritual safety because there is no correction. Proverbs 11:14 says, "For lack of guidance a nation falls, but victory is won through many advisers." There is safety when there is counsel and correction.

You'd think that living in God's will is a walk in the park, but it's more like a walk in the valley of the shadow of death. When I was a kid, whenever I wanted to hang out with my friend down the street, my dad wouldn't let me go until two tasks were completed:

1. Clean room
2. Clean kitchen

And even then, I would have to beg him until he said yes. "Why can't I just go, Dad?" I'd ask, and he never gave me a reason.

I now know that this was discipline. My dad was training me to take care of what was mine and not leave the house in any type of way. We are not held captive, we are not imprisoned, but we do have a standard, and the *world* sees God's standard as jail time. According to God, preparation of His chosen ones means building endurance, and building endurance can feel like long-suffering. We live in a time when long-suffering is rejected, but long-suffering is necessary preparation to lay a solid foundation. The way that will determine your destiny is how you choose to yield your life and if you believe in the God who knows what He has called you to do in your lifetime. My dad *just* wanted to be a father to his child, and he knew that meant expectations and, sometimes, saying no. This can be painful to both the father *and* the child—a father seeing his child in pain but a child seeing the route that they want but choosing to obey the road less traveled. Discipline is necessary.

> For the time being no discipline brings joy, but seems sad and painful; yet to those who have been trained by it, afterwards it yields the peaceful fruit of righteousness [right standing with God and a lifestyle and attitude that seeks conformity to God's will and purpose]. (Hebrews 12:11 AMP)

I could have snuck out and chosen not to listen to my father's commands, but there is power in conviction. The route that we desperately need is the route that God intended—called His will. He gives life, but He also has power over death and decision. He is omniscient, and I believe that He wants to see just what we will do with what He has already given us: life. Will we take the time to be good stewards of what we have? Our willingness to follow His leadership is shown by us walking in obedience. If you decide that you want to control your own life, you will meet chaos sooner or later.

Yielding Through Trauma

When my dad died, I was incredibly broken. My only father was taken away by a so-called "Good God." Where is the *good*, God? I saw the good when my life continued after his was taken. My life was shattered until I saw the reason why. I'd always ask God for more signs that He was real, and He showed Himself to me in an unexpected way. God, why would you allow this hurt to show me? Why would Jesus CHOOSE pain? To show that HE is the Way, the Truth, and the Life. To remind us that God is not the Father of darkness but will turn every dark situation into light. *Jesus did not suffer for nothing.* He suffered because we have a good Father who desired freedom for eternity, offering salvation to every person, leading them all to eternal life if we believe and follow Him. Yielding through trauma requires a high level of endurance and perseverance.

> Then Jesus said to His disciples, "If anyone wishes to follow Me [as My disciple], he must deny himself [set aside selfish interests], and take up his cross [expressing a willingness to endure whatever may come] and follow Me [believing in Me, conforming to My example in living and, if need be, suffering or perhaps dying because of faith in Me]." (Matthew 16:24 AMP)

This may sound unconventional, but I'm glad that I chose God in my grief, and I'm even glad that I grieved. My eyes wouldn't have been opened in the way that they now are. Personally, my heart wouldn't be as available because I would've had an earthly father who loves me enough, so why would I need a heavenly Father? I understand why I need Him now. Even if I had everything, I still need Him. I pray that you get it, too. If not now, then later, but hopefully not too late. He is for us and never against us. When we are choosing the will of God, His goal is not to torture us. Sometimes, it takes trauma to open our eyes, to get our attention, and to answer our questions. Maybe my dad didn't have to go; maybe he could have chosen to take better care of himself, but he didn't. He is gone, and I won't allow weight to follow me, and you shouldn't either, no matter your situation. I choose to believe and embrace that *all* things work together for the good of those who love the Lord (Romans 8:28).

> And He withdrew from them about a stone's throw, and knelt down and prayed, saying, "Father, if You are willing, remove this cup [of divine wrath] from Me; yet not My will, but [always] Yours be done." Now an angel appeared to Him from heaven, strengthening Him. (Luke 22:41–44 AMP)

Selflessly Yielding

Love is passion without boundaries. Love goes the distance, whether times are good or bad. Love is not just a verb or a feeling; it's a burning conviction to be better. Even in the worst of times, love betters. It's not a "feeling" that betters; it's a leading. Attempting to become full of love requires becoming less of self. I have a challenge for you: Begin to live a selfless life. When you walk past people, you either leave a sweet fragrance or a stench. In order to walk in sweet love, you must ask yourself these questions: Where did this response come from? Am I reacting from a place of what *happened* to me? Am I playing the victim or becoming a victim? Your identity stems from a place of what happened or what occurred, but you have the ability to turn this response into acceptance of love rather than rejection of self.

If you want to continue to outpour love, you must become *selfless* and aware. When you were assaulted, how did you start acting after the act? When you were bullied, who did you start bullying? When you were rejected, how did you begin to react? The love we give can only reach as far as our experiences, but our experiences shape our response. How can we respond *without* the trauma greatly influencing our responses?

> *Our experiences yield to our response, and our response is developed by our posture.*

Love is a war between our experiences and our reactions, and it's time to choose an unbiased love. We can only know love well when we extend forgiveness to ourselves and release the experiences that caused trauma. We are not bound to what happened to us. We are not victims of the accuser, nor are we slaves to any slave master.

3 ways to become free of bondage from trauma:

1. Renewal: Renew your mind by understanding that you have the opportunity to not let past experiences

dictate your future.

2. Response: By changing your response to trauma, you can become free from a defeated mindset. Try responding in love instead of out of your emotions.

3. Reset: When you experience discomfort, you are experiencing a test; reset your perception of what it was "supposed" to be.

> I have told you these things, so that in Me you may have [perfect] peace. In the world you have tribulation and distress and suffering, but be courageous [be confident, be undaunted, be filled with joy]; I have overcome the world. [My conquest is accomplished, My victory abiding.] (John 16:33 AMP)

There is likely pressure surrounding you, and you are reading this book because maybe all the chaos is overwhelming. You're trying to figure out why you got married, if you can handle this class, when you'll finally have children, when you'll be able to finally transition to the upgrade, when you'll get the callback, or if you will ever be loved better than the way you are. Love commands answers. Love is not quiet; love is *always* speaking. *Are you listening?* What is love saying today? We are looking for answers when love is sitting right in front of us.

Don't get caught up in what may have hindered love. The tests were not meant to confuse you; they were meant to build you. What were you told? What were you passionate about? What were you good at? What have you lost? You feel far from love because you feel far from the truth that trauma has covered. When we view our current state as insignificant, we become reliant on what seems to be reality because we have a distorted view of what it was "supposed" to be. Even misunderstood moments matter. For example, when I was eleven, I was told I would be an author. The exact words were, "There's a book in you." I was eleven, and the only thing I could think of was when my period was coming and if my crush would notice me. At the same time . . . I was a writer. I would journal my feelings, write poems, talk to my future self, and talk to my mom through handwritten notes. I was constantly creating a story that hadn't been written. Ever since the age of eleven, I've been looking for where the book would come from.

"What situation do I write about?"

"Where will the experience come from?"

"Will I be able to finish it?"

I *never* felt ready. Even as I write now, I still don't feel "ready." Fear is a call to love. Love allows us to be active even when we reject it, even when it doesn't make sense, even when *people* reject us, and when our past hinders us from present readiness. There is no magic age when you are suddenly "ready," but there is a *pace* to obedience. If we pursue love too fast, it can be dangerous, but if love is hindered, it can be damaging. The consequence of being hurt because of loving too fast will show up in the heart of your responses to pain. Where are your responses rooted? Where was love hindered? Why doesn't love feel pure or authentic? What is your pace of love and the heartbeat of healing? Whenever we move too fast, we are eventually shown why we needed to slow down. Whenever we move too slowly, we are shown why we need to move quickly toward love. Love always gives us another chance. That chance comes with an opportunity to tweak what caused us to arrive here.

> *The solution to a lifestyle of questionable love is to brush off the sense that you will always be rejected by love.*

You have permission to lean into the causes of love's pace; love is in your yield.

> We have come to know [by personal observation and experience], and have believed [with deep, consistent faith] the love which God has for us. God is love, and the one who abides in love abides in God, and God abides

continually in him. In this [union and fellowship with Him], love is completed and perfected with us, so that we may have confidence in the day of judgment [with assurance and boldness to face Him]; because as He is, so are we in this world. There is no fear in love [dread does not exist]. But perfect (complete, full-grown) love drives out fear, because fear involves [the expectation of divine] punishment, so the one who is afraid [of God's judgment] is not perfected in love [has not grown into a sufficient understanding of God's love]. We love, because He first loved us. If anyone says, "I love God," and hates (works against) his [Christian] brother he is a liar; for the one who does not love his brother whom he has seen, cannot love God whom he has not seen. And this commandment we have from Him, that the one who loves God should also [unselfishly] love his brother and seek the best for him. (1 John 4:16–21 AMP)

Season 5: Green

Human Nature (Efficient to Grow)

Opposing forces and insufficiency have ways of teaching our heart's roots the most valuable lessons.

*G*reen reminds me of nature. This color gets us back to our original design and our Maker. Green ignites a remembrance of money, nature, and nutrition. In this chapter, we dive into the many aspects of our nature.

I remember the times when I'd wait so long to eat that I'd feel light-headed. My stomach would start to feel uneasy, and I'd be mad at everyone because *I* decided not to eat when I needed to. I'd get mad at everyone but myself. "Gracelyn, can you help me?" Me: "No, I don't want to." "Gracelyn, did you . . . ?" Me: "No, I'm out of energy." "Gracelyn, you need to . . ." Me: "Don't tell me what to do." I responded this way because I was *hangry*. I was angry because I was hungry, so it resulted in me not completing tasks because I decided not to give my body the nutrition it needed. When we do this, we tend to miss the call from our body informing us of what we need. We have every form of control to care for ourselves, but we blame everyone else for what *we* didn't do.

Feeling spiritually empty means that we're not consuming food to fuel our system.

We're depriving ourselves of nutrients, which can lead us to starvation. If you're filled up with addiction, sad love songs, alcohol, clubs, friends that drain you, and lies from your own (consumed) mind, it's time for a cleanse. You're filled with negativity because either you starved yourself or you filled yourself up with junk. How do you get out of this state if you've consumed junk? Purification. Purification is in the purge; Jesus is in the filling. Purification is the cleanse that your body needs. Jesus is the bread of life. It's normal to crave junk, but it's lazy to consume with no discipline. You lack discipline because you don't practice productivity. You stay complacent because junk food is comfort food. You don't have faith because faith doesn't look comfy; it's not as pleasing as the world's options. Spiritual nutrition is consuming your Bible, talking with others about how good it is, digesting revelation, and watching God nourish you. We are most productive in God's presence.

Faith is like a muscle. Exercising faith means that you are exercising discipline. Sometimes, it means blindly leaning on a promise that only your faith is sure of, but your flesh doubts. You're putting in the work now only to see results later. In the world we live in, delayed gratification doesn't seem appetizing, but it's necessary. Energy presents itself when your body gets used to the routine of discipline. When we begin to run toward Christ with clarity, momentum, assurance, and joy, we find ourselves energized. It's no longer about appearance; it's about if what is on the *inside* of you is healthy, holy, acceptable, and pleasing to

Christ. THEN your outer body will line up and look like the Chicago River on St. Patrick's Day: green and vibrant. *What are you consuming?* You can be in great shape, but are you in great health? For most of my high school life, I struggled with cardio in gym class. I was always one of the last to complete the mile. However, when anyone mentioned weight and physique, it was always, "Girl, you're a toothpick." This narrative impacted my ability to show up confidently, and I became so focused on how I looked that I no longer functioned to *be* healthy—I just wanted to *look* healthy for their approval. Just because I was slim, they assumed that I was healthy (and I was), but I still wasn't able to function with as much speed or agility.

This is the time that we live in. We are a generation that wants to appear to be healthy, but in actuality, we are not. Everybody is different, and your run may not look like theirs, your shape may not look like theirs, your talk may not sound like theirs, but you know your body's ability. Your consumption may be different depending on how disciplined *you* are. God never designed us to compare ourselves to others but rather to raise the standard over our own lives and meet our own goals. If our goals overflow to recognition, great, but if our growth is based upon recognition, we have been consumed by vanity. Purity is muscle memory—the more you exercise goodness, the more you'll look like it. You may miss a few days, but you can't be gone for too long; otherwise, you'll lose your figure and your desire to pursue a healthy lifestyle. Discipline produces nourishment and nutrition in ways that can expand our ability to see clearly and give grace abundantly. Your life is fuel efficient, and it's time to run off functional nutrition.

Giving and Gaining

People are priority, which often means that the "pure-hearted" decision is the one that is sacrificial. I knew what I had (or didn't have) in my bank account when I sowed into someone else's life financially, but I also knew what God prompted me to do. It can feel like negatives triumph over positives when you are led by God. I say this to say when you give, there are after-effects. In giving, you may experience one or more of the following:

- It hurts because you know your limits.
- There is a loss that you feel the need to fill as soon as possible.
- You don't understand how you're negative because you were just positive. In other words, why are you suffering when you just did a good thing?

In giving, it can be uncomfortable because you may be making a personal sacrifice for the benefit of another life. Whether it's monetary, time, or energy, giving is sacrificial.

You know that you are *pure* in giving when:

- You give with no complaints, regardless of what you have.
- You give with joy (God loves a cheerful giver).
- You WANT to give.
- You give without expectation of a gift in return.

You will always be refunded for insufficient funds if you call on the Father of all situations and seasons.

> Remember this: Whoever sows sparingly will also reap sparingly, and whoever sows generously will also reap generously. Each of you should give what you have decided in your heart to give, not reluctantly or under compulsion, for God loves a cheerful giver. (2 Corinthians 9:6–7)

The Nature of Generosity

Maybe you have this mindset that when you give, you should receive something in return—you *expect* a thing. Truly, this is the way that I treated God for so long. "God, if I do this, then you should do this." But this is how the relationship really works:

"God, I'm going to do this because I want You to be glorified." We think what we give equates to what we get, but *works do not determine faithfulness*. There are times when our giving yields return with rewards, but our faith should say, "I will be faithful because God is good," not expecting anything in return. Luke 6:38 says, "Give, and it will be given to you." Tearing down the "law of attraction" when it comes to God doesn't make Luke 6:38 untrue, but it allowed me to serve God because I *wanted* to, not because I wanted *something*. As you live and give, you'll notice that God will bless you *either way*. We don't have to beg and plead for God's goodness or gifts.

Out of hopeful reciprocation, we begin to expect something from others because we gave to them. But have we thought that they may not even have the capacity to give to us in ways that we gave to them? What if you're in a season of giving, and they are in a season of receiving? We must be mindful of the assignments that we have been given and not become bitter when the outcome is not reciprocity or exchange.

Hope deferred is a cyclical ride of unmet expectations.

> "Hope deferred makes the heart sick, but a longing fulfilled is a tree of life" (Proverbs 13:12).

Imagine God being conditional like us. A certain level of expectation is good; it's a part of faith, but when it comes to people and giving physically, spiritually, and emotionally, expectation can produce bribery and can easily turn into manipulation in order to "get" something. Don't forget that you will be blessed, but this might just be your season to serve. In the same way, you are not a revolving door that people can just use and come in and out. These are moments to ask God and discern what your assignment is and where you have been called to position yourself. Discern if you are giving out of a place to fulfill your lack or giving in obedience.

The Art of Giving

Imagine you are in a relationship. You are giving your all—serving, loving, praying, and dedicating. Despite all your intentional efforts, this person is not reciprocating. You would probably ask, "Do they love me? Do they care?" You went above and beyond, but you did not receive the same treatment. Love is patient, love is kind. This means that the foundation of a relationship is not only giving but also receiving to experience the gift. Give yourself a chance to receive gifts, blessings, and efforts.

Give *of* yourself so someone else can receive. At the same time, learn to receive from the Father rather than giving up because the other person didn't follow through. Trust me, you'll get it back—sometimes in a different way than you gave, but that's okay because love is *considerate*.

> *The art of giving tears down selfishness and pride, posturing you to naturally reject offense and bitterness.*

The nature of good character is considering how the other person may receive best and giving out of the abundance of one's heart. You sacrifice not only because they sacrificed for you but because you desire to love this person through sacrifice, regardless of what they did first. Receiving can be uncomfortable because you don't always receive the way that you thought you would, but you can open your hands once you've opened your heart in obedience. This is the approach to being rich in giving, receiving, and sacrificing.

> *Be the humble part of humanity.*

Here's an interesting fact: "Filaments of fungi intertwine with the tips of tree roots to form underground networks that seem to benefit both organisms: the filaments, called hyphae, break down minerals in the soil that trees can then take into their roots, and the fungi get a steady supply of sugar from the trees." Something that we might perceive to be harmful has the ability to produce. Something that doesn't seem attractive benefits the living things around it. God has the ability to restore, recycle, and consume all of humanity. Just as trees and fungi work together, what you think has the potential to destroy you is producing you.

> And we know [with great confidence] that God [who is deeply concerned about us] causes all things to work together [as a plan] for good for those who love God, to those who are called according to His plan and purpose. (Romans 8:28 AMP)

A Negative (−) Plus a Positive (+) Equals (=) a Negative

Math tells us that if we do something positive, it can result in a negative, right? It cancels my positive out? I'm surely no mathematician, but consider this and pay close attention to the parenthetical signs: In giving, it can be uncomfortable (−) because you are making a personal sacrifice for the benefit of another life (+), yet it *seems* you haven't reaped the benefits of your giving.

Wait . . . because the reward is coming. Give without expectation of receiving; give and, hypothetically, throw the receipt away so you won't be tempted to look at the price you paid. Give with cheer and love without measure or wage. Sacrifice with souls in mind, endure the negative account so that you may never find yourself there again. Always aim to have enough so that you may give again. Not only monetarily, but in every way, give recurring love, and never cancel the subscription of love no matter the cost.

Here are ways to be or become rich in giving:

Financially prioritize. Get a little; give a little. In other words, schedule to take care of yourself but plan to give. Fill your spirit up, *then* pour out to the next generation and your neighbor. Make sure to let people know that they are a priority in your life.

Ask God for wisdom, and find ways to be a blessing.

Mentally consider. Always consider others.

Physically serve. Serve others before yourself. As you feel led, go the extra mile to help a heart.

Emotionally detach. Cut off your emotions, and give through generosity, not greed or guilt. Give with no strings attached. Never mention what "you did" for them; giving is not about keeping a record of what you gave or when you gave, but more so *how* you gave and how it benefited the person you gave to.

Spiritually give. Give in wisdom. Be obedient in giving. Give with no regrets.

If you don't give financially, you always have an opportunity to give mentally, physically, emotionally, and spiritually. Consider daily how you give. When the prompting to give is clear and confirmed, do it with joy in your heart and follow through in obedience. In your marriage, friendships, job, and society, giving should be a standard principle.

Prosperity is wrapped up in the principle of giving, and when we give, we prosper with priceless gain.

Nature of Fear: Refreshing Your Perspective

The refreshing comes when you cut off the branches of what *was* and tend to what is and is to come. In my childhood, my family would take road trips from Chicago to Mississippi to see my grandparents. After twelve hours, we would enter the long rocky roads with the tires rumbling against the gravel. The roads were pitch black, with only the truck headlights illuminating each couple of feet. When we drove through the darkness, I always noticed the trees towering above the car. The darkness overshadowed the beauty of the eighty-foot trees on what seemed to be the longest roads in history. There were no streetlights, no homes with lights on—just a family on a journey trying to see the next turn. These massive trees always made me think of giants. I was scared the trees would get up and start walking toward me. Even crazier, I thought a zombie man was going to come out from the trees and leave us for dead in this dark forest. Funny, but true. It's interesting where your imagination can go when you're afraid. Sometimes, when you're in a dark forest, you can't rest until you arrive at your destination. The questions of life become, "Will I make it out alive? How long will it take until there's freedom? Will I be separated from love?"

Truthfully, these giant trees did not have legs. Once I started looking past the forest trees at the stars, the trees didn't seem so scary anymore.

> *When we only see what we're surrounded by, we feel consumed by our environment.*

There is always a way out. I remember waiting until the morning when I could see that the fear I'd been consumed by was only maximized because of darkness. Typically, fear is just an illusion of darkness. We see this giant problem, and it becomes 120 feet bigger than what it is. If only you had light, you would see the beauty in nature and not fear the giants. For me, in the morning, everything was okay. Let me tell you, in the morning, *it will all be okay*. I know you want to hear that it'll be okay right now, in the shadows and in the darkness, but I want to show you how a morning light can shine on a dark night.

Perspective Ownership

When merging hope into darkness, we must see darkness as a simple illusion or a distortion of truth—placing emphasis on *illusion*. Your circumstance can be changed through what I call *perspective ownership*. There is a view that you're seeing that could be valid but also distorted due to the fear of what could happen. Open your eyes to the light, and breathe in the unwavering truth that whatever this giant is, it is *already* defeated. I'm not only referring to people or the co-worker or even your own thoughts. I'm talking about speaking things that you want to believe rather than speaking what you see with your natural eye.

> (As it is written [in Scripture], "I HAVE MADE YOU A FATHER OF MANY NATIONS") in the sight of Him in whom he believed, that is, God who gives life to the dead and calls into being that which does not exist. (Romans 4:17 AMP)

> For our **light affliction**, which is but for a moment, worketh for us a far more exceeding and eternal weight of glory; While we look not at the things which are seen, but at the things which are not seen. (2 Corinthians 4:17–18 KJV, emphasis mine)

What if I told you that the battle you're facing is light?

In order to conquer the giant, you must take ownership of what intended to bring you harm.

Again, this is not taking ownership or control of people; this is taking ownership of your perspective.

You can't have a miniature mindset when you are a giant facing a miniature illusion.

In my preteen years of visiting Mississippi, I got tired of always arriving with fear. Instead of closing my eyes and clenching my teeth the whole ride down the dark road, I released my muscles to ease and relinquished control. My inner dialogue of control went from "The trees have power, so I won't look at them" to "The trees are teaching me something, so I'm going to stare until there's no more fear." Defeating fear requires your strongest, most natural form of self to show up. When there's a spiritual battle, you don't fight it with your flesh; you fight it with your belief and the sword of God's Word. After I recognized and identified fear, every ride down to Mississippi on that long, bumpy road became *perspective ownership*, and I looked up at the trees and exposed the lie by looking at fear head-on.

Are there still some little girl fears? Yes, but even my uncle says that the trees still scare him sometimes. In our humanity, it doesn't matter how big you are in stature; it matters how big you are in spirit.

Next time you recognize fear, look up at the trees and envision yourself being bigger than the object. In spiritual battles, boldness intimidates the enemy *every time*. You cannot conquer a battle while thinking you won't win.

> *The battle that was intended to harm you is the same battle that will consistently show up to cleanse you from a defeated mentality.*

The truth is, we never lose. Even when you're scared, imagining everything that could happen, or longing to be out of the darkness, you never lose unless you surrender to the darkness. Unless your heart surrenders to the shadow and your mind yields to defeat, **you never fail**.

In the dark Mississippi woods, the roads never made it easier. They were winding, twisting roads that felt like they never had an end. Have you ever felt like you're on a dark, winding, twisting road that will never end? I felt this a lot, and I allowed life's circumstances to toss me around. I realized that when our perspectives shift, we begin to see how many are fighting for us and with us. How many angels went before us to ensure protection through the forest? You realize you're almost there, and the distance is only a tool to build your stamina. You notice that you had family who lived on this road the whole time, and even if you ran out of gas, you could just get out and have a home. You have never been left or forgotten. You have never been left to die. You have never been alone to the point of having to make decisions without God's voice and guidance. You have never had to carry all the responsibility with only your strength. You have never been obligated to tend to battles, wounds, and scars when you're wounded yourself. You have never been God, and God does not ever expect you to be God. It's time to take ownership of your perspective.

> "Listen carefully, I have created the smith who blows on the fire of coals And who produces a weapon for its purpose; And I have created the destroyer to inflict ruin. No weapon that is formed against you will succeed; And every tongue that rises against you in judgment you will condemn. This [peace, righteousness, security, and triumph over opposition] is the heritage of the servants of the Lord, And this is their vindication from Me," says the Lord. (Isaiah 54:17 AMP)

GOD created the smith and the weapon, but they will not prosper against you. Interesting, right? Why would God create something that has the potential to harm us just to say that it won't prosper against us? Well, it all comes down to if we truly believe Him. He created the weapon, but He wants to show us that HIS nature is good regardless of the opposition we face. We are not in control, and there is a destination that He is journeying with us toward. We must believe that we are protected. "Ye are of God, little children, and have overcome them: because **greater is he** that is in you, than he that is in the world" (1 John 4:4 KJV, emphasis mine).

In your nature, there was never an expectation on you to be a savior. There was only a call to own your perspective. What is intended to hurt you never can once you take *perspective ownership*. The repercussions of defeat yield to something even greater than yourself. Even the trees have a God. Even your enemy must submit—even that fear bows to something. **Are you taking ownership of your perspective?** If we came to God like children, we could also come presenting our bruises to our Father.

"Look, Dad, I hurt myself."

"Look, Dad, someone hurt me."

"Dad, do you have healing balm? Because I'm tired of the bandages."

Knowing that there's a present Father can help alleviate the pain of the fall. *Humanity Shifter*, God is with you.

Trust Fall: Facing Fear Even When You're Safe

In our human nature, we tend to find issues. Once one thing happens, another happens, and once that thing has been dealt with, then we're on to the next. We are constantly fighting with forces that seem so beyond what we're capable of defeating. Faith is not a call to comfort; it's a call to risk and trust.

> He said, "Come!" So Peter got out of the boat, and walked on the water and came toward Jesus. But when he saw [the effects of] the wind, he was frightened, and he began to sink, and he cried out, "Lord, save me!" Immediately Jesus extended His hand and caught him, saying to him, "O you of little faith, why did you doubt?" (Matthew 14:29–31 AMP)

The truth is that you *are* protected; however, risk *can* be a call to safety. When you fall, you know that God will catch you, but when you surrender, you have no idea what will happen with your trust. We'll call this concept the *trust fall*. When we're safe, there's an abundance of assurance, but when we're yielded, there can be an abundance of fear. Why is that? We can only comprehend as far as we know, and when we don't know, we don't understand. This is a call to take the most rewarding risk of your life and *trust fall*. Allow the battle to cleanse you instead of wound you. Stop giving your heart faster than your integrity.

Stop making excuses to yield to unhealthy patterns before you evaluate where the unhealthy pattern came from.

Cleansing is coming for you, but there needs to be an urgency in discovering *who* you are trusting and *what* you are falling into.

Here's an exercise: Write down who you are trusting and what you are falling into. Be honest with yourself; acknowledge what you struggle to trust God with and what you are not fully falling into Him with. Do not be ashamed; just be honest and ask yourself, "Where do I struggle to trust fall? What do I cling to?"

_____

_____

_____

_____

_____

Now that you've responded to where you struggle to trust fall, it's time to rush over your shortcomings with truth. Let's be

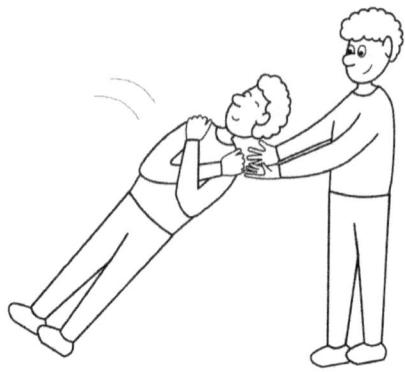

honest, you messed up. You didn't respond with love; you abused someone's trust. You are looking for the result more than you are looking to God. You have a hard time loving the most important person in your life. You became dependent on people and distant from God. You rely on your own strength and willpower to accomplish everything. You're never "good enough" for God, and the list goes on. Friend, we *all* fall short (Romans 3:23). There is no perfect way to live, but there is a way to be cleansed. Cleansing is like the smell of spearmint—crisp, clear, and refreshing. The "spear" that "meant" to harm you is now the spear that you use to demolish every lie, break down every fear, and build up truth. Owning it means choosing it. What are you owning, and were you ever meant to take ownership?

> Put on the whole armour of God, that ye may be able to stand against the wiles of the devil. For we wrestle not

> against flesh and blood, but against principalities, against powers, against the rulers of the darkness of this world, against spiritual wickedness in high places. Wherefore take unto you the whole armour of God, that ye may be able to withstand in the evil day, and having done all, to stand. (Ephesians 6:11–13 KJV)

Allow God to tend to the garden of your heart. Lean back and trust in the One who withholds no good thing from you.

Season 6:
Yellow

Joy Comes in the Morning (Alive in Christ)

*I*f joy comes in the morning, what do I do at night? Why is there a need to hide just because there's shade? Where is your hiding place at night while you wait for the morning?

After being assaulted, I realized that I had gone into hiding. I hid from myself, I hid from others, and I hid from God. Typically, when we face trauma, we are tempted to hide due to shame. This hiding affects our souls. Our minds go into places that hide from the storm; we hide from the truth and deny the very thing that has us take responsibility, and our emotions are all over the place whether they are stored or shown. There is an internal desire to hide your faults and expose your greatest ability. You fight with the fear of healing and the reality of running. I remember running from my hiding place to get to another, but I realized that only *one* hiding place is safe, which is in the secret place.

> He that dwelleth in the secret place of the most High shall abide under the shadow of the Almighty. I will say of the LORD, He is my refuge and my fortress: my God; in him will I trust. Surely he shall deliver thee from the snare of the fowler, and from the noisome pestilence. (Psalm 91:1–3 KJV)

Sunblock

> *We are just children who want to play out in the sun but keep forgetting the sunblock. Here's what you do in a season of sunblock: You put on your sunscreen and sit in the sun with the Son. We are called to block the shade of rebellion.*

When I hid in the shade of pornography addiction, my insecurities became my security. When I nestled in the arms of my relationships, my problems were dealt with. When I gave my image to social media, I was accepted by the numbers. We tend to hide from the reality that we need to confront. When I kept running, I kept hiding. There was a day when I got so tired of the desire to be seen, known, and accepted by people that I decided I could do it all for myself.

I could achieve, and if I could achieve, then I would raise the standard, and if I raised the standard, I would be seen, known, and loved in spaces where I needed no help. Self-sufficiency became what sustained me. My capability became my crutch. Oftentimes, we are running from the one hiding place that we need to be running to. Sometimes, we run so fast that we forget to see if we're even running on the track. Emotionally, I was so drained that I knew I needed to confront what I was running from. It was love. I was running from love because if I discovered real love, I might feel unworthy or rejected. I also feared that if love found me, I would reject it. Rejection of love will never build love; it will only distort it.

Love is meant to carry and support the weak areas that we can't manage on our own. The same relationships, arguments, and feelings about myself and the same cycles of stagnancy kept happening. There was a moment when I stopped running away from God. I simply remained where I was placed. Eventually, like a yellow sunflower, I began to smell the fragrance of my life. I began to see that there was meaning to the life I was running from. Purpose became real, and perspective became accessible. I was no longer double-minded, but I was now seeing myself as God saw me. He just wanted one thing—me. But the one thing He wanted, I rejected. So "me" was always the hardest to give.

> *Our flesh will naturally resist the urge to pursue Christ, but there comes a time when your soul gets weary of resistance.*

The urge to reject God is the same urge that causes dysfunction.

At fourteen years old, I was forced by a female to indulge in sexual acts that I did not want. The after-effect left me confused, even though I had always known who I was. When we get a taste of sin, even if it's forced upon us, we can start to believe that sin is better than salvation. The truth is that opposition comes to keep you bound, and freedom seeks to keep you in the light. There are moments when your life may feel like a tug-of-war, pulling and battling for where you belong, making you think you should just let the other team win. The thing about tug-of-war is that you usually have teammates to help you; you don't have to win alone. I realized I was blinded by a reality that was determined to keep me bound, but now I'm facing the truth that I have been found. I was never hidden from God, and neither are you. Sometimes, we're so blind because we make up excuses for why we can't see, and taking off the blindfold exposes us to the light. I had a deep desire to see, and *sight* is what protected me. I could see that I was blind. I was walking in the shade, desiring to come out of sinful behavior, but the fear came when I didn't know what I was coming into. It's a process.

Maybe for you, the shade isn't lust or confusion. Maybe it's rejection, mental illness, self-hatred, self-sabotage, gluttony, anger, or insecurity. When stepping into light, the fear of failure can hinder you, but when you finally take the step to expose sin, you see that exposing *yourself* is no longer necessary. Walking in the light means that perfection no longer comes from *your* power but from God's Spirit. Grace allows us to be free, but we need guidance. We do not want to enter the world exposed; we want to enter the world protected. Everyone has access to protection because it's free, but there's a payment that comes with the pursuit. When opening our hearts to healing, it makes no sense why we trust the process—healing is all in *who* we trust. When you are first starting to heal, there's no proof of success; it's just that *trust fall*. After that trust fall, we need to be nourished by the sun while we're down. Falling into the loving arms of God is falling into the One who knows you best. There is something within you that He is pursuing, and you must be open to the pursuit. You don't have to know it all; you must simply become reshaped by the protective, trustworthy God who wants to revitalize you through His Son.

> Then I went down to the potter's house, and saw that he was working at the wheel. But the vessel that he was making from clay was spoiled by the potter's hand; so he

made it over, reworking it and making it into another pot that seemed good to him. Then the word of the Lord came to me: "O house of Israel, can I not do with you as this potter does?" says the Lord. "Look carefully, as the clay is in the potter's hand, so are you in My hand, O house of Israel." (Jeremiah 18:3–6 AMP)

The Source of Light

It's not every day that we feel empowered to press through. In our human experience, there's often more darkness than light, but we need light to be lit. We cannot live dim, soaking in the darkness all around; we must live with a spark. Although you may not feel like you have that light, it's already inside of you, and nobody can dim the light that shines from within. Maybe you've never faced depression or a deep sadness, but I'm sure that you have been in darkness, needing light. You know how you go to the bathroom in the middle of the night searching for the light switch when you've known where it was located for ten years, but it's dark, and you're feeling around for it? You're tripping on air on your way there even though you are in a familiar place. This shows how human we are physically and how reliant we are on light—something that we actually come from. Can you comprehend how much spiritual help we need? How much guidance is required to go from point A to point B, even in a familiar place—home, work, school, church, coffee trips? (In my case, tea trips?) How do you find light when it's dark? We must keep our lamps burning. Luke 12:35–37 instructs us: "Be dressed ready for service and keep your lamps burning, like servants waiting for their master to return from a wedding banquet, so that when he comes and knocks they can immediately open the door for him. It will be good for those servants whose master finds them watching when he comes."

When we lose the light that calls us, we lose the reason why we burn, why we're "on," and why we exist. Losing sight of this causes us to go into a dark, downward spiral. We begin believing the lies of our desolate minds. It causes us to lose our affection for the things that matter most. Let's get to our "lit lives"—the lives that are operating on nothing but pure life *because* of the light.

I would define my lit life as one where my light is never dim, and my spirit is always trimmed and burning. It's a life where people look at me and say, "Wow, Jesus lives in her; it's undeniable." I need to live an undeniably dedicated life to Christ. My life must come without question that I am the person God called me to be before the foundation of the earth. My lit life is one where my family is at peace, and my heart is still. That's the lit life that I strive to obtain daily. It's okay if I'm the quietest in the room, figuratively hidden, or not quite what I thought I would be by now. As long as I'm living a lifestyle that's holy and acceptable to God, it's lit.

How would you define your lit life? Reflect on something that makes your life worth living. What sets you apart from the crowd and brings you joy even in the darkness?

_____

_____

_____

_____

_____

When our light goes dim, we need a sensor. We *need* a sensor. This is why determining your *lit life* is imperative. We need guidance beyond what the world or politics or social media have to offer. In a blackout, you can try to keep walking in the dark, but a flashlight would make it much easier. Spiritually, the ultimate sensor is the Holy Spirit. He is the twenty-four-seven guide for humanity. In Season 3, I said that God is three in one. He is God (the Father), Jesus (the Son) in human form, and the Holy Spirit is the road map, guiding and helping us daily to be more like Christ and pleasing to God. The Holy Spirit helps us live because we are tripping (literally, figuratively, and spiritually speaking). The

Holy Spirit is the sensor, and God is our help when we can't help ourselves. He is the guiding light at all times. 1 John 1:5 says, "This is the message we have heard from him and declare to you: God is light; in him there is no darkness at all."

The Source of Energy

Maybe you've been exposed to sunlight and felt the warmth on your skin, and your energy and hope returned, only to go back inside and return to that sick bed. What we fail to realize is how much nature calls us toward itself. We are being drawn into a healing power every breath we breathe as our body is constantly fighting for us, regenerating itself. The question is, what are you being filled with? What is nourishing you? What is your oxygen? I'm referring to the daily, seemingly harmless tasks. For me, that thing was validation. If I conformed to society's offer, maybe I could be accepted, but I never knew that I was *already* accepted. When I gave God access to myself, my senses opened up. I couldn't shine on my own; light shines best when surrendered to a reflection. Whether or not we've identified what that light is surrendered to, there's only *one* safe hiding place, and it's not in the shade of our flesh.

God's Hiding Place and Sin's Shade

God's hiding place is:

- Safety
- Trust
- Genuine
- Certain
- Vibrant

The shade of sin is:

- Harmful
- Deceitful
- Manipulative
- Confusing
- Blinding

If we enter a safe hiding place, we have entered shelter. When you are in the arms of the Father, there is only safety and never harm.

> "He who dwells in the shelter of the Most High Will remain secure and rest in the shadow of the Almighty [whose power no enemy can withstand]" (Psalm 91:1 AMP).

God's hiding place is a preparing place for the future, but in this place, the shade of sin can deceive you into thinking that the hiding place is a lonely place. Shelter is not lonely; shelter is safety. At times, we reject what is good because we believe that we can get away with bad behavior. What if God withheld blessings when you were "bad"? The school "gold-star system" did not set us up to succeed. We were taught that things were withheld when we didn't behave or produce at a certain level. The way that life really works is even when someone is not behaving well, that person can still end up on top. *Why*? Whether you are in the shade or in safety, you are abiding in *something*. Although Satan is evil, he still has a kingdom with a strategic agenda. Satan is defeated, but he's still shooting arrows, attempting to make sin look good and shelter look unappealing. We experience this in society daily. Fake is praised, and authentic is snarled at. Do not think because you're in your hiding place, people who are in the public eye are obedient because they seem to be blessed.

There is much striving when you toil to be seen. When you are hidden, your posture is set up to strategically put you in places you would have never seen if you toiled for attention. I'm not referring to fame or fortune; I am referring to an unshakeable inner joy that I call *internal wealth*. You become rich only when you become submitted to the one Sovereign hiding place. When you go away, sit still, and remain quiet, you dwell with the One who created the sun, the shade, and the hiding place. It's all a test to see what you will choose, where you will dwell, and what you will do when it's time to be seen. Are you living your life for credit or for Christ? We were not created to perform or strive; we were created to be more like our teacher (Jesus)—this does not always yield earthly return. In Christ, we have eternal pleasure, which is the hope for humanity.

Are you satisfied? What shade have you decided to sit in? Where have you pitched your tent? What is pouring out of you? We like to think we're better than we are or worse than we are, but when we develop a moderate, healthy view of ourselves, we can see with sober, clean eyes *who* we are.

Even if we sum ourselves up to nothing, the problem is still not solved. It is not you who lives; it is Christ who lives in you. Therefore, whether in the shade or the hiding place, there is grace for you. Sometimes, we place sinners in the shade (deeming them to hell) and saints in the safe hiding place (based on our judgmental perception) to make ourselves of something. We do not sit in the judgment seat, so we must be careful who we judge and who we hold in high regard. We will *all* be judged, and we are *all* on a journey. Self-righteousness puts us in the judgment seat when we're called to walk in humility and be meek and hidden. Being hyper-focused on others' sins or successes tends to blind you to yourself and your own developmental journey. We are all dealt with, taught, developed, and trained in places where we abide. Share love, stand for unity, and leave judgment up to God. At the end of it all, there is one righteous Judge who sees all and knows all. There is a grace or a standard on each of our lives to walk in the calling we have and steward it accordingly. Maybe you're not called to fix anyone; maybe you're simply called to abide with your Maker so that love and light can transform those around you.

> Enter by the narrow gate; for wide is the gate and broad is the way that leads to destruction, and there are many who go in by it. Because narrow is the gate and difficult is the way which leads to life, and there are few who find it. (Matthew 7:13–14 NKJV)

> So I, the prisoner for the Lord, appeal to you to live a life worthy of the calling to which you have been called [that is, to live a life that exhibits godly character, moral courage, personal integrity, and mature behavior—a life that expresses gratitude to God for your salvation]. (Ephesians 4:1 AMP)

Authentic Light

My dad's laugh was the third loudest thing about him; the first was his scent. He smelled like walking essential oils—not just one but all of them. Frankincense on his right wrist, clove on his left. Cinnamon in his hair and peppermint on his chest. The second loudest thing was his style; his walk was hip—an upright posture with a little bounce. His talk was direct; it never beat around the bush in hopes that you'd feel better. His fashion sense was like style was in his bones. He could wear all the colors of the rainbow and still match from head to toe. My father was like the color yellow, leaning in with joy (sometimes too much to take in all at once). His joy was like a flash of lightning, lighting up the lives around him.

There was a day when I was feeling very tired and down. My body felt depleted, and that trickled into parts of my spirit. I'd planned to go to a worship night to not only support my former high-school assistant principal and his wife but also to take note of what they had to say on the topic of marriage. When I saw the flyer, I planned to go, but it was one of those plans that wasn't set in stone. It was four in the afternoon, and I needed to leave in thirty minutes to arrive on time. Truly, if I don't feel ready in my soul before I'm ready, the chances of me going somewhere when I'm already undecided are slim. I wasn't feeling well; I was cloudy in the head, and I only had so much time to get out of bed. Finally, I made a dedicated decision, saying, "Lord, I am going by faith, so You have to carry me and have Your way." I went to this worship night, and it was beautiful! I was so excited to catch up with people I care about, and I left on this beautiful sunny evening wanting to go out on the town. So, I found the pasta place that I loved, and I ordered carry-out.

I walked into the Italian spot, and the young lady at the register had nothing less than an undeniable joy. All I heard was *joy*, and I could tell she was an extrovert. The light she emitted caused me to feel *inferior* to her joy. I felt like it couldn't rub off on me, though, because, well, today just wasn't my day. Although the worship time had lifted my spirits some, I was still dragging. When it was my time to purchase, joy found me. She asked questions, and I responded. I "put on" a smile because I began to feel God helping me through this dull moment. The joyous cashier and I ended up connecting on social media, and I left that place fired up with joy—fireworks on the Fourth of July type of joy! I had a new walk, a new talk, and a new sound. It was like she was anointed to carry joy just for me at that moment. I got in the car and wanted to get right back out and conquer the city. Literally, nothing could stop me. Remember, I became clear with God before I left, saying, "Now, Lord, You listen to ME. I am going for YOU, so have Your way," and HE DID, and it benefitted ME! I was wearing yellow nail polish with a colorful red, yellow, and blue striped shirt. Yellow was the color that popped, and it complimented my nails.

What was the name of the only person I had hugged at the worship night? I'm glad you asked. Her name was JOY. Little did I know, I'd experience the meaning of her name the very next hour of my life. Truly, God embodies all good things, even in seemingly meaningless or insignificant moments. The joy in yellow just cannot be taken away; it cannot be undone, and it cannot be moved. Joy unspeakable is who the Lord is. So much joy that you can't even speak. For me, it was joy "can't stop speaking," so I called my mom, sounding like I'd had a Red Bull, five cups of coffee, a shot of sugar, and two Baby Bottle Pops. I was inspired again and on fire again, and it didn't happen by request. It happened by faith, prayer, and supplication. Your breakthrough is on the other side of your faith. Amidst the chaos of life and all that you're feeling and experiencing, joy is never too far away.

Lemon Scone

Joy is like the lemon scone that my dad left for me because he knew I wanted what he had. I found my joy in the little thoughts that my dad expressed daily, like when he stroked my chin and said, "Look at my baby," or when he spoke of the beauty of my almond-shaped eyes. Dad was the only one I believed; when he said it, nothing could counter what he knew about me. Joy is one beat out of the hundreds of heartbeats in a day. You must hold on to it; remember that it came, it mattered, and if it weren't for that beat, you wouldn't be at this one. All things matter; it's all significant and purposeful. Choosing Christ in your dark moments will light up your life. In my experience, joy is what I'd always desired. Some would consider joy a smile, a bountiful amount of energy, or a brightly colored shirt. For me, joy is really a rainbow peeking through a rainy sky. I have found that joy is not always a smile because smiles can be fake. Joy is not always laughter because laughter can betray. Joy is not always color because color can hide the dark feeling inside.

We live in a culture where shares and likes are more desired than hugs. The truth is that real connection is joy. *Authenticity is joy.* Emotion is not always joy—contentment is. The rejection from others tends to rip contentment away, but the production of joy is not found in a man or a woman; it is found in knowing that God sees you when nobody else does. Joy is meekness. Joy is the revelation you receive when you ask God for a sign. Joy is not shallow. Smiles can be cunning, laughs can be inauthentic, but *joy* is authentic. I believe that every human has a naturally joyful expression. Where is the real you? Don't let anyone dull that natural sparkle. When we pretend, we go home emptier, but if we just show up *authentically,* our *joy may be contagious.*

The pursuit of joy is a daily one. It's the place that yields not to opinion but wisdom. Joy is only good when it comes from the Lord. Otherwise, you're just thriving off emotion, good vibes, and a good time that will eventually run out, leaving you to strive again next weekend. The danger in temporal happiness is we begin to lose our sensitivity to the things that matter most, needing another thrill. Strive to find joy alone, unattached, and in solitude. We can't unify authentically until we carry authentic joy. With lackluster joy, discernment becomes compromised for the sake of agreeing. The person in the corner of the room is left out because they don't function like you, and inauthenticity is at an all-time high.

> *Joy is inclusive, joy is aware, joy is united, joy is solitude, joy is correcting, and joy is uncompromising for the sake of the gospel.*

If it's not joy, it's likely not thriving. We are called to *thrive*, and thriving does not always come in the form of knowledge or a smile. Thriving comes in the form of a human like you who has a transformative effect on the world around you. Where is the childlike version of you who enjoyed your style, had your own interests, and stood for what was pure? Don't suppress who you really are; let joy breathe again.

Many people don't have authentic joy; they have suppressed joy from trauma, pain, and their past.

Let's dive into a joy assessment:

Has your joy been suppressed? If so, what caused the downfall of joy, and why did you let joy go?

___

___

___

___

___

What is your expression of joy, and how do you express it authentically?

___

___

___

___

___

There's joy in the mundane awaiting you today. Whatever you do, don't neglect the joy that is right in front of you.

SHIFT HUMANITY

Season 7: Orange

The Heart's Fire (Healing the Wounds)

Orange. The color of fire. The color of freedom. The color of power. When I see fire, I see freedom. I see sin burning and salvation brewing. I feel an unrelenting warmth, and it's so warm that I feel a chill. One of the purposes of fire is to bring light in darkness. The Father has the ability to set you on fire. This is a part of His personality. The Christ-follower is purposed to figuratively set souls on fire for the gain of heaven. I call this *spiritual pyromania*. A pyromaniac is someone who is obsessed with starting fires. They literally can't stop themselves. We must become a people obsessed with reason and purpose.

We are spiritual pyromaniacs. We are set ablaze to become fire starters. You have the tools to ignite the world around you today.

Creation on Fire

God is the creative one who gave us creative ability. We are not that smart. All things were creative before we began putting price tags on creativity. He is a stroke of fire, ignition, light, and truth. Before I was set on fire by God, I was in a dull space—one where you try to fit in everywhere but just can't find your place. One where you try to pursue God and do right, but you feel nothing is happening. A place where all your "friends" go out without inviting you. The place where sickness doesn't seem to go away, and grief doesn't seem to weigh less. This place is similar to the season of black, with the reality of darkness surrounding you. Initially, being set ablaze can be uncomfortable and isolating. It's equivalent to this: no friends, no fun, baffling, frustrating, and burning with passion, just to name a few.

I only got out of this shade by doing something different. I lived outside of the norm and did not compromise. This place is one of refining. The quietest places are the ones of great production. They give us space and time to be alone with our thoughts and original ideas. Don't consider the quiet seasons meaningless. Consider the quiet seasons as times to make meaning. There will come a day when you will see that you were set apart to be the difference. You can't be different surrounded by the same people.

So, be the friend at home, watching your friends having a great time without you. Be the one who is misunderstood. Be the one who people ignore at the event. Be the tired, single family member who's still in process. Be the things that are unconventional so the whole of Christ can live in you. This is your time to produce. *Let the fire consume you.* How? Understand that holy fire won't burn you, but it will ignite you. Friends will come, relationships will bloom, anxiety will cease, and sickness will die, but you will still have to face something—the reality of being set on fire to ignite change in the world around you. It's not the kind of fire that's typically desired; it's the fire that fights through temptation, consumes confusion, and breaks comparison. It burns away dysfunction and stands for truth. To obtain the fire, you must first be processed for it. Maybe you've always wanted to burn for something with substance. You can start right here, right now. Start with this prayer:

> God, set me on fire. Fill me with Your Holy Spirit. Help me to have uncompromising faith. I accept Your consuming fire in my heart, in my sight, in my speech, and in my conduct. Jesus, work in me and through me. I give You permission to creatively work with my hands and within my soul. I desire to go higher in You and pursue the lifestyle that You have predestined, regardless of what meets the natural eye. Lord, show me Your truth, distract

> every distraction, light my way, and light up my life. In Jesus' name, Amen.

When I prayed this prayer, I began to gradually come into a knowledge of what I was made for. This fire will take you to new levels in Christ. Your level may not look like those around you, but there's a spark for you.

The fire is the spark in you to walk through trials when it would be easier to walk away. The fire is passion to walk through the valley for the sake of someone else. The fire is the long-suffering that you endure because there are refined people on the other side of your obedience. Have you found freedom in the fire that was meant to kill you? Did you take the initiative to persevere when the pressure was hot and heavy? The question is: Have you ever been in the fire? It's so hot that it's cold. It's so red that it's orange. It's so bright that it's blinding. *This is Christianity.* Christians are called to be walking fireballs, but far too many Christians have a blow torch. When you are on fire, not only do you look different, you *are* different. It's okay to not be socially accepted; it's okay to not follow the trends. It's okay to go through hardship when it seems everyone else is thriving. Don't be afraid; walk like you carry endurance. *Father, ignite the fire.* In the good and the bad, let the fire never burn away. It's for your good.

You must submit to [correction for the purpose of] discipline; God is dealing with you as with sons; for what son is there whom his father does not discipline? Now if you are exempt from correction and without discipline, in which all [of God's children] share, then you are illegitimate children and not sons [at all]. Moreover, we have had earthly fathers who disciplined us, and we submitted and respected them [for training us]; shall we not much more willingly submit to the Father of spirits, and live [by learning from His discipline]? For our earthly fathers disciplined us for only a short time as seemed best to them; but He disciplines us for our good, so that we may share His holiness. For the time being no discipline brings joy, but seems sad and painful; yet to those who have been trained by it, afterwards it yields the peaceful fruit of righteousness [right standing with God and a lifestyle and attitude that seeks conformity to God's will and purpose]. (Hebrews 12:7–11 AMP)

Strength in Dependence

Fire is a conundrum and can bring with it warmth, healing, or danger.

We need heaven's fire because we are human. We need strength and healing. Have you ever seen a cut heal? Have you ever seen a scar fade away? Healing is proof of God's compassion. If cuts never closed, we would be at risk of diseases and sickness; if the gut didn't exist, we would never be able to uphold the wellness of the human body. We were created to heal. Healing is the evidence of God's existence. You cannot deny Him when you have seen His miracles—at least you'll have questions. If it were up to me, nobody would ever feel pain, but then, what do we live for? The tension of burning offers us dependence on God and gives us an opportunity to take our pain somewhere. We either heal daily, or we try to justify our scars by covering them up. What are you covering the scar with? Have you ever had a cut and put alcohol on it to help it heal? It *burns*. Even if it's as small as a paper cut. I remember watching my family's reaction when I put hand sanitizer on immediately after I got a paper cut. I did it so that I didn't have to prolong the healing process.

There is no way to be covered without once being exposed and uncovered. Here's the number one way to remain in the hole that you feel you've been in: Have you ever said "I'm okay" to someone when they asked if you were okay, but you really were not okay? It's as if this response is second nature to the human experience. This is a stellar way to remain stuck and unhealed. If it burns, it burns, and that's okay. It's not realistic to always be "okay," and it's okay not to be okay because not being okay can truly lead to healing if we let it. Faking a smile is the hardest thing to do; it's like pushing a cart that won't move. There is something between a lie and truth called healing. Healing begins with identifying the issues that were ignored. Instead of repetitively saying, "This is just who I am" and "Cut me some slack," I found myself releasing with lots of tears rather than holding back due to the fear that I knew would come with vulnerability. God brings warmth to hardship. He brings a stabilized security in knowing that where you are and what you are living in today is awakening you. Spiritual burning *is the awakening of our inability to control our lives.* When the winter comes, and the wind is as frosty as winter blue and as frozen as white ice, the fire is there to keep us warm—wrapped in the blanket of His arms in the middle of a sweltering summer day. It is the compassion that we delay because we don't seem to need covering on a summer's day, so we opt for comfort. We'd rather burn in the freedom of the sun because feelings feel better.

Humanity is passionate; we were created to want more. We must choose if we'd rather burn for Christ or burn in hell, and these are options that many would rather opt out of than consider. We don't want evil, but we don't want good either. The world has come to a place of compromise for the sake of pleasure; people think an upgrade has something to do with their works. Yet, an upgrade obtained in sin is inconvenient.

A lack of desire to burn for God is a call into struggle, not strength. Strength is not based on independence; strength is the art of dependence on God, which yields obedience. We tell our lovers our secrets and bask in the comfort of illusion; this is called delusion. Secrecy is not freedom; sin is not freedom. When we play with fire, we eventually become burned by it, then consumed, causing danger. Simply put, sin is dependent co-habitation with everything and everyone but God.

Weakness needs something to support it, so is strength pride? We must humble ourselves in dependence so we won't be burned by unhealthy independence. When I hear, "You are so strong," my response is thank you, I'm devoted and dependent. This should be our posture. We must not become accustomed to taking credit. Are you healed from trying to be strong alone? The truth is what we *should* set our eyes upon, and the lie is oftentimes what we *feel* like setting our eyes upon. My most valuable strength never comes from a Pilates class or the gym. It comes from burning in the secret place. When you discover the middle ground, acknowledge the urge to take credit, and actively choose dependence on God, you have started your journey toward purification. There are times when I'm upset and crying and just want my mom to answer the phone. When she doesn't answer, there have been times when I've felt weak. There are simply times when I desire guidance. Humanity needs help; we need *healthy* company. There is nothing wrong with healthy dependence, especially when we are surrounded by a multitude of wise counsel. Because of our humanity, at times, we look for comfort in the world and not the Creator of the earth. And we try to be strong alone because independent strength looks better than dependent weakness. He stands with open arms whether we seemingly need Him or not, but we tend to run to Him only when the conditions are cloudy, windy, icy, or freezing. What if we ran to God when we didn't feel the need for His fire, healing, or strength? He will set you ablaze when you run to Him in the midst of a winter's night and in the calm of a beautiful summer night. He wants it all. It's okay to be refined, defined, and purified through dependence. Become weak and let it burn.

"Where there is no [wise, intelligent] guidance, the people fall [and go off course like a ship without a helm], But in the abundance of [wise and godly] counselors there is victory" (Proverbs 11:14 AMP). Who are your fire starters (mentors, counselors, pastors, etc.)? Who in your life starts good soul fires and helps put destructive ones out?

_____

_____

_____

_____

_____

Now, identify who or what puts out your fire. Who or what in your life drains you? Who doesn't add biblical foundations and truth to your life? Why do you still have them around? Identify fears and why you feel those people or things are a necessary safety net:

_____

_____

_____

_____

> The eye is the lamp of the body; so if your eye is clear [spiritually perceptive], your whole body will be full of light [benefiting from God's precepts]. But if your eye is bad [spiritually blind], your whole body will be full of darkness [devoid of God's precepts]. So if the [very] light inside you [your inner self, your heart, your conscience] is

> darkness, how great and terrible is that darkness! (Matthew 6:22–23 AMP)

Here are the ways that *you* can defeat the enemy with fire:

Look at yourself. When you get some time alone, go to the nearest mirror and stare at you. This can be an internal mirror or a literal mirror. Simply take a moment to look at yourself. Looking in the mirror gives you an opportunity to see any lies hiding in your own eyes. Once you stare into the face of the thing that has tried to cover itself up, you will see the truth through your broken eyes. The eyes are the lamp of the body, and we must look within to heal.

Ask yourself:

- Who am I?
- Who do I want to be?
- Where am I headed?
- What am I here to accomplish?

Before I began living with Christ, I had many "breaking sessions" where I looked in my internal mirror and saw the lies that I had bottled up. I told myself: "You are not good enough, you have no money, you are below average, your family isn't proud of you, you're too slim." Now, I have the tools to reject all these things, but not then. I knew the enemy was trying to overtake me with destructive fire. After staring at *me* day after day, there were some things that broke that needed to be mended—and it wasn't the mirror. It's okay to dig deep to be refined.

Target the truth in you. Tell yourself how much you don't understand why that abuse happened to you. Tell yourself how you could have prevented that accident. Tell yourself how you could have listened to your parents. Tell yourself how "no" would have been the better answer. Tell yourself the truth about your feelings and your reaction to the world around you.

Now, pause. Breathe in and out, and release the guilt, shame, doubt, worry, and every anxiety. You targeted the truth, and now it's time to love yourself enough not to ignore it. There is healing here and now.

Have patience in refining. You've looked in the literal or internal mirror, you've told yourself the truth, and you've breathed, but you still feel like you're one step short of the goal. Or maybe this exposure made you feel like you've taken a step back. *You must have patience.* Anxiety is a lie. Failure is a lie. These are the lies we just tore down and will not go in a cycle because it's not happening in your timing. Let the fire refine you.

Let's be the *Humanity Shifters* who:

- Face the truth. (Be bold enough to pursue the cross through the chaos.)
- Look in the mirror. (Be wise and come face to face with limiting beliefs.)
- Tend to the heart. (Be willing to be refined from within.)

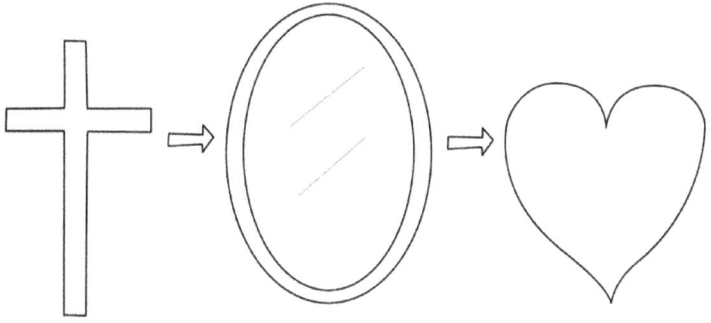

Patience lies in knowing that the process is inevitable. You are progressing, you just don't feel it because YOU had:

- A plan
- A deadline
- A goal

God has a plan that you are called to trust in the middle. Do not let the fire destroy you. We are consistently pursuing a new process, a cycle that is out of our human control. Only God has control of what you tried to take upon yourself. HE has:

- The plan, the process, and all the details
- The deadline
- The goal
- Protection over your life

Destructive Fire Tactics

While in the process of healing, know that Satan wants you back. When the holy fire consumes you, Satan will try to get you back to your old way of life to destroy you. This is the spiritual battle. You may see every lie, downfall, and breakdown, and the things that you prayed against are the things that will come to test you. The things that you prayed FOR now seem further away because you have a distraction called, wait for it . . . temptation. Temptation is a tactic bound to happen, but don't give it power or attention. What we will give temptation is the fire. In this case, the heat is a firm and certain answer called a *decision* because when temptation comes, we have decided that *our strength is in our dependence.* Maybe YOU don't feel strong enough, but the fire of God IS your strength.

> *When destructive tactics come, constructive plans prevail.*

We have the Father so that we don't have to use our own strategy.

> Therefore submit to God. Resist the devil and he will flee from you. (James 4:7 NKJV)

> No temptation [regardless of its source] has overtaken or enticed you that is not common to human experience [nor is any temptation unusual or beyond human resistance]; but God is faithful [to His word—He is compassionate and trustworthy], and He will not let you be tempted beyond your ability [to resist], but along with the temptation He [has in the past and is now and] will [always] provide the way out as well, so that you will be able to endure it [without yielding, and will overcome temptation with joy]. (1 Corinthians 10:13 AMP)

> And I say to you that you are Peter, and on this rock I will build My church; and the gates of Hades (death) will not overpower it [by preventing the resurrection of the Christ]. (Matthew 16:18 AMP)

> For the wrath of God is revealed from heaven against all ungodliness and unrighteousness of men, who by their unrighteousness suppress the truth. (Romans 1:18 ESV)

Constructive Plans

To get stronger, we exercise.

Here is an exercise to train your mind to use strength in the tempting moments. Remember: We war not against flesh and blood but against spiritual principalities (Ephesians 6:12). We are not fighting against people; we are fighting the enemy operating in them. We are not fighting situations; we are fighting the temptation to sin.

In a case of temptation, when an evil spirit entices you to go to the club, your response is . . . no.

In a case of temptation, when an evil spirit suggests that you get the number of someone you know you shouldn't, your response is . . . no.

In a case of temptation, when an evil spirit curses at you and attempts to tear you down, your response is . . . no.

In a case of temptation, when an evil spirit attempts to seduce you, your response is . . . FLEE.

On a normal day, temptation is difficult, and on a hard day, temptation seems impossible to flee. But this will allow you to exercise strength in the power of your response so that in those moments, you will remember that "flee-dom" is possible.

> *"Flee-dom" is the act of fleeing from temptation in every moment in pursuit of freedom and fire.*

Do not "match the energy" of the enemy that's attempting to tear you down. Instead, keep your peace, remain strong, and use wisdom.

Wildfire Awareness

Sometimes, life can feel like an out-of-control wildfire, bursting at the seams with questions and concerns at every step. We must continue to burn bright and endure the heat. Bursting with abundant life means burning with holy fire.

I recall a time when I was furious. I had so much anger boiling inside of me that I couldn't even find the words to say. With veins popping out of my head and my nostrils flaring, I was searching for the response within me that could put out this internal "fire." Passion is good, but a proper response, through controlled burning, is necessary. "A gentle answer turns away wrath, but a harsh word stirs up anger" (Proverbs 15:1).

Our inability to notice and accept that we are flawed affects our perception of outcomes. We will always play the victim if we believe that other people are the reason why our lives are a certain way. Have you considered your response? Have you *deeply* pondered how you sounded when you reacted? Sometimes, we are blinded by our fire because we never intended to start it. Our intention was never to hurt, harm, or use, but because of the pain of the past, we set up a defense to never be abused again. This can show up as unintentional manipulation or narcissism. In my last few years of mentoring and coaching artists, public speakers, influencers, and ministry leaders, I have found that *everyone's* reaction to a present circumstance is rooted in past offense, trauma, or experience. It wasn't until we walked through identifying and healing that they overcame it. I can attest that I have faced this in several areas of my life. Introspection is not typically human nature's knee-jerk reaction.

When I realized I was affecting people with every move I made, I realized that *I* was the drama. It was *me* causing discomfort and causing people to tiptoe around telling me the truth. I was who I was, and you could not tell me who I wasn't. Here, in the presence of safety, just me and you, here's the truth:

> *You will never run fast enough to escape truth.*

You can try to outrun what you need to acknowledge, but eventually, it will all catch up to you.

At fifteen years old, when my brother sat me down to tell me that life was not about me, I was incredibly offended. I cried, I made up excuses as to why my voice should be heard, and I even deflected. How does this really sound? Someone who I knew loved me was biting his tongue out of love to protect my heart, but his frustration was built up, so he exposed the truth in me and to me. Love confronts, love pursues, and love burns. My flesh was burning with fury during that conversation as he told me to "just listen" as I was over-talking. I felt unheard, unseen, and uncared for; I was fighting a battle with no defender. At least, that's what it looked like to me. If my brother had not sat me down that day, I would have never realized what God was trying to burn away. God was setting me ablaze for an awakening wildfire that never burns out. I call this awakening *wildfire awareness*. Wildfire awareness is when you recognize that you affect the world around you. *You have the potential to either build up or cause damage to entire communities, people groups, and lives. You must harness this fire.*

Now that I'm aware, I can't escape asking what I've done, how I could do better, how I sound, and if I offended with my tone. I now attempt to listen as opposed to defend. If you want to *Shift Humanity*, work on the part of you that is tempted to be heard and just *hear*. Listen to correction, and above this, ask God if there is offense in your heart. The truth really does hurt, but the truth also sets you free.

In what ways are you exercising *wildfire awareness*? What are your reactions to others? What's the last bit of correction that you received? Are you containing yourself or lashing out?

_____

_____

_____

_____

_____

> So Jesus said to the Jews who had believed him, "If you abide in my word, you are truly my disciples, and you will know the truth, and the truth will set you free." (John 8:31–32 ESV)

Refining Humanity's Fire

There is no greater love in the world than exposure for the sake of a *refining*.

To be refined is to be defined. How can the fire that attempts to consume turn into a fire that fans the flame? Well, you lean into your *unique ability*. We were all born with a personality—including facial expressions and maybe even a "clap back" or "crash out" ability. Your personality is not bad in and of itself, but we tend to direct our energy in the wrong ways, which can cause others to be offended. Do not mistake your feelings for failure. If you feel anger, maybe you are called to bring harmony or justice. If you feel sadness, maybe you are called to encourage. If you feel envy, maybe you are called to unite. If you feel hurt, maybe you are called to heal. Your feelings may be valid, but they need redirection of energy. God has a way of giving beauty for ashes. The danger in accepting your feelings rather than expanding faith is that we only see one side and one way. If you look at the heat waves that come from a burning fire, they extend to something beyond our sight. *Where do those heat waves go?* If we notice that there is a flip side to our feelings, we will be able to see that faith wants to take us somewhere. It's time to be refined. Trade your weakness for a new wave of glory. There is immense simplicity in trusting God with our emotions; it's a wave of compassion that empathizes with us yet defines us fairly. The One who is worthy already knows what we struggle to give; He even hears your whispers in the night. God is our defender. Keep whispering, and before you know it,

His glory will come and show you what you've waited for. The fullness of His presence produces healing in the heaviest places of our hearts.

> In this you rejoice, though now for a little while, if necessary, you have been grieved by various trials, so that the tested genuineness of your faith—more precious than gold that perishes though it is tested by fire—may be found to result in praise and glory and honor at the revelation of Jesus Christ. (1 Peter 1:6–7 ESV)

Let's consider healing to be the product of knowing God in a deeper way. Let's not confuse healing as a destination but rather a resource. Healing is just the path, not the way. Why is this important? When we begin to consider healing as a way to be closer to God, we become attached to a narrative that you're only as good as your healing process. This is false because even in falling, we are loved. So, what makes a process of healing special? It's the ability to understand that the healing was never your burden because you're already healed in God's sight. It's just a part of your job to walk it out.

> *God takes us and teaches us so that we can give Him glory, not so we can abuse what He's done and compare it to souls still in process around us.*

The truth is that healing will not be forced upon you, but you have the choice and responsibility to be refined. None of this happens without the fire!

Season 8: Gray

The Fog in Faith (Anxious Faith)

SHIFT HUMANITY

*W*hen you can't see anything and nothing makes sense, where do you go? When you don't have access to love, and you've lost everyone you trusted, what happens then? Satan has strategically attempted to stop your progress. If only he can get you to stop growing, he can get you to stop glowing. In 2020, I remember watching the news when America went on lockdown, and President Trump ordered all to stay inside due to COVID-19. People were dying, scared, frantic, and clueless. This was a time when my mom, my brother, and I had just moved to a different part of town. All we knew was that we were in this *together*. Most of that year, we would go to the store together, masked and gloved, trying to hold our breath as soon as we walked out the door. All we had were devices, phone calls, and board games. Life was gray. We couldn't see ahead; all we knew was where we were. We came face to face with the reality that control was not ours.

When faced with opposition, we have the opportunity to confront what we do not believe. Hidden spaces are exposed, and broken pieces are constantly falling or mending.

In the midst of the fog, prayer is sometimes our LAST resort instead of our first resolve. I get it: Practicality is closer than prayer. However, without prayer, we just add more chaos, side effects, questions, and harm. We dig a deeper hole. But prayer? Prayer is effectual and fervent—it actually *works*.

> Therefore, confess your sins to one another [your false steps, your offenses], and pray for one another, that you may be healed and restored. The heartfelt and persistent prayer of a righteous man (believer) can accomplish much [when put into action and made effective by God—it is dynamic and can have tremendous power]. (James 5:16 AMP)

The reason mankind struggles with prayer is because mankind struggles with people. Social anxiety, unhealthy patterns of friendship, abuse, fatherlessness, and motherlessness—the list is never-ending. If you could never trust your friend, how could you trust a Father you can't even see and THEN be crazy enough to actually talk to Him? If you have been let down by family and friends over and over again, how would an invisible Father do any better? We tend to build up pride when we limit God—acting as though He is not sovereign enough to redeem and restore what was lost. I'm careful of who I consider a friend because people are faulty. People can betray, lie, cheat, steal, and abuse. The Father calls us friend, and He has plans to never, ever harm you (Jeremiah 29:11).

This is why prayer is essential. Prayer is the call that lets you hear the voice of God. Prayer is both the genesis of and the production of an intimate relationship with God. We don't pray from a victimized space; we pray from a place that yields raw feelings, emotions, requests, and declarations by faith. Prayer is blind faith—talking to the air and being crazy enough to expect a response. *Prayer is the activation of faith.* We must activate our prayer life if we want to see through the foggy seasons.

I have a challenge for you: Pray now more than ever.

Let's start here. **Pray out loud and declare this with me:**

> God, I come to You with all that I have. I don't have much to offer, but I do have me. I ask that You help me through the pressures of life that seem impossible to conquer, and I pray that You'll help me persevere. Father, I need full reliance on You even if I don't fully understand the world around me. Help me to see what I can't and heal where

> I'm hurting. Forgive my sin and cleanse me from the pressure and pain of my past. I declare that faith has made me well, and I believe by faith that I will see the reason for my days. I acknowledge Your perfection, and I receive that You've made no mistakes with me. Help me to see You rightly, and help me to understand who You've made me to be. Thank You, Lord, for Your sovereignty, Your presence, and Your forgiveness. Thank You for loving me and healing me in the deep, unseen places. In Jesus' name, Amen.

What are you pursuing? What you vow to now will determine where you go during *and* after this life. Life or death. Heaven or hell. You can choose defeat or accept victory, but victory is only obtained through the blood, and the blood is applied in the dark and dull seasons. These seasons are shaping you because you were made for more, and you are a *Humanity Shifter*.

An Empty Container

The danger of not knowing where to go is that we become a container for other people's suggestions. The truth is that God has a path planned, and if we fail to heed that voice, we could easily fall into meaningless lies. You will only know if you are in God's hands by where your feet go. Maybe it seems like your feet are on great ground, but is this where *He* set your feet? You will only know when you surrender. In the unknown, there is no way to go back; there is only forward, so what you give your energy to next is preparing you to be a container so you can receive from that season. *What are you containing?* Being a container means having the ability to embrace and release what you hold. If you are living day to day and have no sense of what you're holding, then what exactly will you give?

"A container is any receptacle or enclosure for holding a product used in storage, packaging, and transportation, including shipping. Things kept inside of a container are protected on several sides by being inside of its structure."

Containers were created to hold things. They can hold new food, old food, hardware, vehicles, or storage. Different types of containers are made to hold different types of goods.

> *Evaluate what you hold in your heart, and determine if this is what you'd like to contain.*

Take a few moments to reflect and respond. What are you holding in your heart? What's in the capsule of your heart's container? What is your heart thinking today?

> For as he thinks in his heart, so is he. "Eat and drink!" he says to you, But his heart is not with you. (Proverbs 23:7 NKJV)

Thriving in Rest

We live in a time when productivity is not praised, but performance is. It's a sad reality to know that our world has come to such a low moment when solitude and rest are secondary and not necessary.

> **We know what the world prioritizes because we know what the world contains.**

The truth is, we need rest. I do not mean sleep. We need the sustainable rest that God gives. We need the kind of rest that contains what is good. We are people who need light and need to cling to the light placed within us. There is a generation arising that will understand that rest is not secondary; it is primary. When you wake up, rest. As you walk out of the door, rest. When you go to the grocery store, rest. On your way to the hospital, rest. There is a rest that requires a relationship with our heavenly Father, and when we choose to sit in moments of rest, we choose to sit in the presence of reason. This means that whether we're overjoyed or overworked, there is hope because rest is only a breath away. This mindset combats the fog of anxiety and panic. You might be asking, what exactly *is* rest? I define rest as *the reclining of a moment*. With rest, there is no reason to toil or strive. Take a deep breath, relax your shoulders, and just *be*. Everything will be okay.

To recline means to "sit or lie in a relaxed way, with your body leaning backwards." And think about it, if you're leaning back, you must be leaning on something—supported by something. Imagine God being your back support. Imagine a life where even when the sun is blinding, there is still direction, and you are somehow still able to move forward. Spiritual sight does not mean you can see perfectly; spiritual sight means that you are *intentionally* directed. We live directed by love. I'd like to challenge you to lean back in order to be fully supported. (Remember the trust fall?) This doesn't mean to stop tending to the garden of your heart and life; it means to start letting go of what you thought the garden should look like or produce.

I assume you aren't exactly where you want to be. Maybe you don't have the house, the credit, the friends, the children, the spouse, the career, or the credentials that you'd like, but guess what you *do* have? The ability to be directed. This is what it means to lean back. There is a plan for you, and the plan is good. Nothing can forfeit this plan unless you decide you don't want to yield to it. Rest and yield in the shadow of the Almighty God.

This will turn the gray spaces into grace in your process. When you can see, you have no worries because you know where you're going. When you can't see, there is no certainty—it's all a gray cloud. I'm so happy to announce that we were NOT created to live without vision.

> "The hearing ear and the seeing eye, The [omnipotent] Lord has made both of them" (Proverbs 20:12 AMP).

What's Clouding Your Judgment?

Let's evaluate what might be prolonging your process. It could be your *position*, your *perspective*, your *people*, or your *pride*.

Identify which one of these areas is keeping you in a gray season.

If it's your *position*, you could be feeling like you're in the right time but the wrong place. If this is the case, consider taking a moment to ask God why you are where you are. There's much value in evaluating your position.

If it's your *perspective*, you could be experiencing moments of doubt, confusion, misguidedness, and discomfort. There is a possibility of needing to discover where you have placed your trust. If your mind is scattered, so is your trust. Renew your mind and step into clarity.

If it's your *people*, you need new people. There is urgency in this as people are the building blocks of your life and ways. If the wrong blocks are in place, your entire structure is weak. You need intentional covenant relationships, not just friends that can go out on a Friday night. Yield your mind and evaluate your relationships. Be prayerful about who your people are from season to season.

If it's your *pride*, it's time to tear down the walls that you have built. You are not better than others, and anyone can be broken. Understanding this gives you a level of humility that only comes by learning to love people purely. You are not above reproach, and if you deal with pride, there is grace for you, but you must submit your idea of perfection to the cross.

Gray Zone

A prolonged process is a gray zone that can cause you to be in the wrong *position* with the wrong *people*, producing *pride*, and deteriorating your *perspective*. There comes a time when there is a significant need to rest in the discovery of your process. If you don't have that position yet, don't rush the process. It's better to not have the position than to have a great position at the wrong time. If you don't have the people yet, don't be so desperate that you find yourself associating with the wrong ones. It's better to have no company than the wrong company. (And you always have company with Jesus.) If your perspective is not aligned with truth, don't build up false stories to make it all seem reasonable. It's better to have truth than a short-lived lie. If you are dealing with pride, lean into the submitted lifestyle so that your pride does not bleed into your progress. It's better to have a pure heart than it is to have progress. In the gray seasons, this is a crucial time to see before you are seen. Let go of the circumstances in front of you and trade them for surrender. It may all be out of your control, but there is purpose in the prolonged process.

> For the vision is yet for an appointed time; But at the end it will speak, and it will not lie. Though it tarries, wait for it; Because it will surely come, It

> will not tarry. "Behold the proud, His soul is not upright in him; But the just shall live by his faith." (Habakkuk 2:3–4 NKJV)

Moving Through the Fog

There comes a point in your life when it feels like "it" will never happen. It feels like the money will never be enough, the anxiety will never cease, the spouse will never come, the friends and family will never feel real, or the suffering will never end. The very moment you decide that victory is yours, *it is*. Faith is trusting that victory belongs to Jesus, and He has promised it to you and me. Perseverance is the ability to pursue hope. If you understand that there is a reason for your desire, you begin to understand that the reason for your desire is bigger than the desire itself. Coming into the knowledge of who God is through your reasoning will provide clarity in the fog.

There is a great commission toward understanding the reason for your every move. Why are you at this job? Why are you in that relationship? Why does disobedience make you feel more in control? *What is your reason?* This brings purpose to things that are dormant or things that *need* to be dead. In gray, foggy seasons, we have the opportune time to dive into the motive behind our ability; this motive awakens our faith muscles. When you realize that your why is the driving force of every one of your decisions, you begin to evaluate whether this is a moment that needs life or death. Some of the moments we face do not only need attention, but they also need stewardship. If we begin to steward the fog well, we will be driven toward the light. How do we do this? We follow the truth. Once you determine whether you actually obeyed or not this time, you will see and understand the greatness of a life of obedience. You cannot persevere when you are not yielding. The solution to the spiritual, mental, or emotional haze is abiding in the Father. We cannot see if we are driving with no direction. There is something greater awaiting, but if you're not yielding *before* you get it, you will not be yielded when you obtain it. To persevere is to move toward clarity.

What moves us toward clarity?

There is a time that arises when we get tired. Tired of doing it in our own strength, tired of thinking it will work but feeling like God doesn't even care, tired of going in mind cycles and unhealthy patterns. Your tired is tired, your weary is weary, but the only solution is a lifestyle of rest. When we face temptation, we must rest in truth. In resistance, we rest in truth. In torment, we rest in truth. In discomfort, we rest in truth. In weariness, we rest in truth. Let's lean back and draw close to the one Perfector who knows us better than we can even begin to realize.

Humility says, "I don't know myself well enough to do this alone. I need a Savior." If the kids are acting funny, if your teachers are bullies themselves, if the bullies are consistent, if the adults are persistent in their pursuit of your downfall, if the job is the worst thing you've ever done, if the household feels like too much to handle, if the ketchup got on your shirt in the middle of the meeting and sent you into insecurity, if they look at you too long and you begin to think of what they think of you—there is *rest* for you. Our sense of identity is contingent upon our posture of soulful rest. All the things that have us feeling less than or never good enough or even too much—there is rest for you from God. Did you know that the only thing that you are called to be is loved? You were not called to be a career, a height, a weight, or a look. You were called to love and be loved. This love does not come from desires; this love comes from a Father who knows who you are. You are not a label; you are a loved child just trying to find your way through a foggy moment.

> He lets me lie down in green pastures;
> He leads me beside the still and quiet waters.
> He refreshes and restores my soul (life);

> He leads me in the paths of righteousness for His name's sake.
> Even though I walk through the [sunless] valley of the shadow of death,
> I fear no evil, for You are with me;
> Your rod [to protect] and Your staff [to guide], they comfort and console me. (Psalm 23:2–5 AMP)

How can you prepare for rest?

- Get off social media to enjoy the moment instead of posting.
- Apologize to the person you hurt.
- Have the hard conversations.
- Forgive yourself for the shame that you hold in your heart.
- Empathize with someone's trauma that you ignored in the past.
- Embrace the people you love.
- Embrace the people you struggle to love well.
- Get back to the hobby that helps you decompress.
- Dismantle the identity that you thought came from

your money.

- Enhance your ability to embrace who you are beyond your scars.
- Love the new person that God has called you to become.
- Don't care too much about what others perceive of you.
- Don't care too little about how God sees you.
- Focus on *being* rather than performing.
- Focus on authenticity rather than insecurity.
- Love who you are in the middle of becoming.

Your process is significant, the haze is necessary, and your healing is mandatory. There is a love greater than this world could ever imagine that is pursuing you to completion. Not ONLY will you end well, you will be well. It will all be well—even in the middle.

> *Your process is not inferior to the reward.*

You are greater than the reward because you were created with value and intentional love. Pursue this. Pursue the One who is molding you. The lover of your soul is here to block the shade. Sit under the tree of life. There is something growing in you.

> I am the vine; you are the branches. If you remain in me and I in you, you will bear much fruit; apart from me you can do nothing. If you do not remain in me, you are like a branch that is thrown away and withers; such branches are picked up, thrown into the fire and burned. If you remain in me and my words remain in you, ask whatever you wish, and it will be done for you. This is to my Father's glory, that you bear much fruit, showing yourselves to be my disciples. (John 15:5–8)

Sufficient Memories

My brother went to Mississippi for a family reunion, and I wanted to go, but I couldn't ride along this time. He came back with our family history on a pamphlet going all the way back to my great-great-grandparents. This quickly turned into me digging deep into the past when my mom and I would discuss kingdom leaders such as Kathryn Kuhlman, Joan Gieson, Kenneth Hagin, and Myles Munroe, to name a few. These men and women were evangelists, preachers, and ministers dedicated to faith and serving others. There was so much passion in how they worshiped God in spirit and in truth with song, dance, and joy—passion I don't see today, passion that I desire.

I want that for our nation now. I saw that passionate lifestyle as I remembered my great-grandmother. Her prayers traveled; my GG was a warrior. She always had her stick ready to go. I saw her stick as her defense. I remember riding up to her Mississippi ranch at the end of the rocky road. It was dark. Remember, Mississippi dark is a different kind of dark. The sky is not blue; it's deep midnight with the stars ever so white. On that Mississippi evening, my family and I were inside eating sweet potato pie and every other savory soul food dish she'd made. She grabbed her rod, or in my eyes, her defense, and walked out the back door. Rising from never-ending battles of spades and speed (card games we commonly played), my uncles and cousins followed. She aimed to show us her garden with only the living room house lights to see. We're walking, squinting to see her freshly grown vegetables, and, the next thing I know, she's chopped the head off a snake. I didn't stick around long enough to see it, but I didn't need to see it to believe it was there. I ran into the house so fast as she proceeded to show her garden in the night. She was fearless. I remember her watermelon was always sweet, a different kind of sweet. Her sweet potato pie was the BEST sweet potato pie (you know it's the best when the whole block asks for your recipe). Knowing that she passed away with the Bible on her chest told me that the sweet Holy Spirit knew her even better than I did, and that's enough for me. Sometimes, all we have is a memory, and we're either left with the sweet nothings or the sweet somethings. I remember my GG as a woman of faith.

The memory of the cross is the most significant—a moment endured so we may live life remembering the truth. As you sit and be still in every moment, we are called to recall what matters most; this is the art of *remembrance*. Think about where you are and what you're doing, and produce a spirit of gratitude for your existence. If you still have breath, you still have work to do. One day, someone special died, suffered, and rose to save you. Don't overthink this; let the memories bloom naturally as the field of your gray clouds turns into a pasture that you are led through.

> And you shall remember the whole way that the LORD your God has led you these forty years in the wilderness, that he might humble you, testing you to know what was in your heart, whether you would keep his commandments or not. (Deuteronomy 8:2 ESV)

> I will remember the deeds of the LORD; yes, I will remember your wonders of old. I will ponder all your work, and meditate on your mighty deeds. Your way, O God, is holy. What god is great like our God? You are the

> God who works wonders; you have made known your might among the peoples. You with your arm redeemed your people, the children of Jacob and Joseph. Selah. (Psalm 77:11–15 ESV)

If we live in remembrance of this love, we can navigate our inner world with greater expectation.

Season 9: Blue

Contentment in the Current (Awaiting Joy)

There's a song that lived rent-free in my head growing up. These lyrics by Steven Curtis Chapman played over and over:

"I'm diving in

I'm going deep

In over my head, I wanna be

Caught in the rush

Lost in the flow

In over my head, I wanna go

The river's deep

The river's wide

The river's water is alive

So sink or swim, I'm diving in"

As I would sing this song, even as a young girl, I imagined what life would bring and what Steven meant when he said, "So sink or swim, I'm diving in." Now, I know this to be a declaration that no matter what life may bring, I will remain in the One who is in control of the wind and the waves.

Tossed by the Tide

The discomfort of now is nearly unbearable. You can feel the pressure caving in from every direction and the circumstances of life almost closing in on you. With the state of this world, we have so many waves crashing together at once. Sometimes, we feel tossed and lost in the current. There are times when people will attempt to demean or diminish your season. Maybe they don't feel that your pain or circumstance is valid or worthy to be compared to theirs. Face your season, and conquer this giant like it's one that you were created to attack. Every single age and every single season has significance. If that bullying, assault, abuse, or trauma didn't happen, you would not be who you are today. Every season is necessary, *even* the ones that make no sense to us. New, uncomfortable seasons call for mental, emotional, and spiritual execution. They require a level of stamina that you may not have applied in a different season. In times of training, we are shaped for these kinds of conditions so that when the storm arises, we are prepared. Discomfort is a call to test what you've learned and apply what you've trained for. The Word of God is a sword that prepares us for battle because the Lord knows there WILL be a battle. When this battle comes, how will we respond? Will we back down from hard conversations? Will we have an attitude? What will our disposition be? Will we be angry and sin, or be angry and not sin? It's okay to feel the emotions, disappointment, and pressure of the current. It's not okay to *become* the emotion.

Do not become the bitterness that you feel.

Do not become the sadness that you feel.

Do not become the depression that you're facing.

Do not become the battle you're called to fight.

Become the overcomer you're called and empowered to be.

Seasons of discontentment are pivotal, creating a storm of purpose. Just as the skies and oceans are vast, so is the depth of God's love for you; it has no limits. Additionally, there were no limits to who you were created to be.

There was a season of my life, specifically in high school, when I thought I was only good for one thing. I saw people doing theater, Greek club, fitness club, Spanish club, and all these extracurricular activities, but all I could do was my homework, and I could barely get those answers right. I began to question if this time in my life was worthy to be compared to another, but truthfully, my life was not created to be compared; it was created to be an offering of worship. What I've realized is no matter how many times I compare myself to another, I will never be able to live up to what someone else is doing. Why? Because I'm not them. We all hold a different capacity and desire. I do not have the desire to go on a stage in front of hundreds of people and sing and prance and recite lines that I practiced for hours, days, and weeks to remember. There is no duplicated calling or purpose—yours is unique. Even if we have similar goals and plans, we are not the same. There is a standard in my life that I am living to accomplish daily, and the only reason why I compare myself *ever* is because I have stopped believing that I can have my heart's desire. When we fail to accomplish our goals, we tend to develop a level of comparison that is empty and only produces pride, jealousy, and disappointment. This mindset is dangerous because we begin to act as though our beach isn't beautiful enough because not as many people are attracted to it. California's Venice Beach may be considered the touristy beach, but that doesn't stop locals from going.

There is truly another dimension of grace for you to step into your true design without the thought of the person you might envy or the life you might want. If one person is a rock star being praised by people, but you're an editor who gets little to no credit for what you've created, then I can see how you don't feel as good as the rock star. There are a few things to notice about the rock star to editor comparison: Attention does not mean acceptance, and position does not equate to obedience. Let's lean into this. When we feel as though we are not as accomplished or valuable because of what someone else has the capacity to hold and be, we tend to sink into our ocean. On the shores of our lives are questions, anxieties, pain, and deep envy—even if it's not noticed. Maybe you're not jealous of someone else's life; maybe you're disappointed with your own. There is a light inside of you that shines for the sake of God, not man. If a rock star is getting more attention than the editor, we need to realize what we have become as a society. What do we clap louder for? What *is* the standing ovation for? What is the praise all about, and who does the glory belong to? God or man? This doesn't mean that the rock star demanded attention or respect from the fans (at least not every time). However, there is a level of entitlement that comes with attention. Attention is not inherently negative unless the attention brings praise and glory to self—yes, even if the rock star acknowledges God.

We must be careful with the orphan mentality, thinking that we have been forsaken and only rock stars are seen. This is a misconception.

> *Not everything seen is good.*

There is beauty in leaning into your design when you humble yourself in the valley *and* on the stage. We are only as good as the wave we carry and bring to others. This wave can either consume others and drown them by way of pride or consume others in the love of God. You were created to be different. Your job, salary, journey, home, and family will look different, and that's okay. Your difference makes you special. Attention, fame, and fortune are not good if you are already drowning to be seen. More of anything requires more responsibility. Do not ask for more gain; ask for more grace. When we carry our every season with a tender response, we are able to recognize the weight of the responsibility that we *already* have to carry. There's a gift actively existing inside of you that requires your responsibility. God is good enough right where you are. You are no less than because you don't have the newest car; you do not have to look like them to be accomplished. You are not required to show up as anyone else now or then. Even if there's pressure to do it their way, do it God's way instead. Do not praise the destination when you are in waves that are defining you. What appears to be success doesn't always mean it's successful.

There are times when we feel like our season will never end. The tide takes over and bombards our lives until we feel we're at our wits' end. I remember a time in 2018 when God spoke a word through a prophet (a stranger to me) that I would be living in California one day. At that time, I had dreams and goals of living there, but it was a distant dream. May 9, 2021, came around, and I received a text from my friend who lives in Los Angeles who asked me if God was calling me to move there. At this point, I was shocked but also felt like it was preparation time. I hopped into some trusted Facebook groups suggested by friends, started scouting roommates, asking my community if they had any leads. After countless potential roommate Facetime calls, I started decluttering my room and packing suitcase after suitcase by faith and prepared to head out of my mom's home to make my first move.

At that time, there was an urgency, and I had to stop trying to have all my ducks in a row. The only things that gave me comfort were my mom's prayers and confirmation that God was already impressing upon her heart through dreams that this move was God's leadership. What I feared the most was moving out of eagerness or disobedience due to passion, but with much prayer and consideration, I finally came to the decision that I would choose a date and move. I chose December 6, my dad's birthday. Although I had a date, I told God, "I'm not moving unless I have a job." (Funny how I thought I could tell God what I would or would not do while simultaneously asking for His will to be done.) After going back and forth with what I'd considered to be a dream job at the time, I got a job offer. So, according to the "deal" I'd made with God, it was time to move out to LA.

    I packed my bags, landed in Los Angeles with my mom, and headed to a hotel. I still didn't have any leads on roommates or secure housing, but I was there. I was in the promise. I took the leap of faith and officially lived in Los Angeles, California. I faced the most faith-filled transition in 2021—then I hit rock bottom. The job fell through after a short time, and I was feeling alone, humiliated, and confused. So, I decided I was moving back home! Gently, yet passionately, I heard, "Don't leave, endure." These were the hardest words to hear at that time. I was left alone to decide if this move was about logic or about obedience. I was torn between whether I should go for comfort's sake or stay for faith's sake. I stayed. I was stripped of home, warmth, comfort, and joy. For two and a half years, I held on tightly to my community and leaned on the God who called me to this promise. Although the entire journey was like a heavy wave, I found moments of contentment. I hosted events, built communities, worked for high-level executives, built my résumé, lost friends, gained family, lost money, gained a wealth of experience and knowledge, and most importantly, I wrote the bulk of this very book.

Your season may be confusing, you may be grieving your old life, you may have forgotten what comfort is, and you may have been stripped of everything, but God is producing something inside of you today. There is destiny brewing in you right now. There is an assignment in this season. Joy and contentment are being restored. You may not see it today or tomorrow, but after this season of mourning, after these moments of tense friction, and after this "current" passes, you will see that God is producing something inside of you. As you await joy, find contentment here in the current. It's okay to dislike this season, it's okay if you don't understand, it's okay if nobody else understands, and it's okay if you have questions. It's *not* okay to be stagnant. It's time to produce. Remember Jesus' words to the paralytic man: "Jesus said to him, 'Get up, take up your bed, and walk'" (John 5:8 ESV).

Produce

Throughout my two-and-a-half-year journey in Los Angeles, I had some low lows, but my highest high was when I recognized that I was in God's will and kept going. Although the discontentment came in like a flood, there was a standard that He raised to become my banner in times of the unknown. The banner has always been love, restoration, security, and life. There is no better feeling than knowing that He called us for such a time as *this*. As we produce, we become consumed. This consumption is not full of vain realities or accolades; this consumption is one that lives to produce, not for the sake of gaining glory or credit for yourself. Would you create "it" even if you got no credit or reward? Would you be obedient if "it" didn't benefit you at all? Our entire being was made to worship, and we are all worshiping *something*. For some, the logical mind is highly trusted, or the voice of a friend or family member has too much input, causing a tainted faith. Maybe your trust is more in the perception of man than the goodness of God. Maybe your trust is contingent on seeing the promise first, like me when I told God that I wouldn't move until I had a job. These are possible realities that we all struggle with from time to time, but if you hear His voice, you will understand your pace. How do you hear the voice of God? You seek Him.

His breath in our lungs alone gives us a reason to reject self-glorifying ways. Once we realize that there is purpose to our breath, we can begin to realize that there is life in the mundane—every breath matters. Not one is wasted, and this is what gives us reason to produce. If we are consumed by God, our entire being can yield, and execution becomes easy. Easy doesn't mean there will not be resistance; easy means that you are determined by, through, and in the name of Jesus, and life becomes a dance. There is a strategic production that brings purpose to your veins. There is a reason for the waves. Don't let the waves of life toss you around. Don't let people deter you from God's purpose, but rather, be a proponent of endurance and faith to end well and complete the assignments you're called to produce.

> So that we may no longer be children, tossed to and fro by the waves and carried about by every wind of doctrine, by human cunning, by craftiness in deceitful schemes. (Ephesians 4:14 ESV)

Where Are You?

The purest form of you is the one that applies, commits, prepares, examines, filters, and discovers the *entire* being. Regardless of where you might be, create with the Creator. Leave nothing out of God's sight; begin and end nothing without Him. How do you do this? Create a personal invitation every single day. Thank God for building and producing identity within you that is never apart from Him. This could look like moving a heavy desk by yourself all the way to hosting a million people on a live stream. There is a God named Yahweh who wants to give you the strength to move the heavy desk and give you the grace to host a million people on a live stream. He created the waves and your current, so there's an unstoppable grace for you to produce right where you are.

SHIFT HUMANITY

Creatively, maybe you know what to do when producing, but internally, you may have some trouble in production; let the wave of God consume your limiting beliefs. There was a time in middle school when I was consumed by the perception of others. This mindset was only developed because my friends at the time decorated my locker for my summer birthday. We were in the last days and moments of middle school, and the bullies who seemed to be assigned to make my life terrible ripped all the decorations off of my locker during a passing period and threw it all away. There was only one pink streamer remaining. These girls disliked me for no reason. I was only kind and loving to them, but for some reason, they felt the need to ruin my celebration. This caused me to think that I was never worthy to be cared for, and because of this, all I wanted was to be cared for. So I looked for care anywhere I could find it and anywhere it would be given.

When we look to people for acceptance, we rarely find it. The reason? *The very people you are looking to affirm you are the very people who are looking to be affirmed themselves.* As you chase their validation of you, they're seeking someone else's approval. I began dressing like the bullies to be accepted rather than rejected. I developed a false humility that created a disconnect between me and my identity, so I had to build it all back up in the wave of God's pursuit of me. I did have a desire to be accepted, but I had this understanding that it would only come from and through people because people see me every day, and God doesn't, right? Wrong. He is the God who sees us. When I yielded my idea of being seen by people, I began to accept that the sight of God was enough. He is El Roi, the God who sees (Genesis 16:13). This produced a knowledge in me that love is after me, and I *must* ride the wave. I resisted the wave of love for a long time until I became desperate for oxygen. As we gasp for air in the ocean of life, we gasp for love. My comprehension of love was one-dimensional, desiring the pleasures and acceptance of people.

Where are you? Are you living to please people or please God? People pleasing will consume a part of you that was *made* to be pursued by love. Love desires to pursue you. Do you want to be consumed, or will you continue to run from truth? Which is greater, being noticed or just *being?* We were created and designed to produce in purpose beyond the results and despite the tension of life's waves. Producing in obedience causes a pure perspective, which, if we're after, has the ability to create the greatest *Humanity Shifters* of all time.

Take a moment to evaluate where you are.

What keeps you going?

What are you producing?

What waves are crashing against your production?

Who is discouraging your progress?

What has God spoken to you that you feel is beyond your ability?

Do you fear any moments in the process of production?

_____

_____

_____

_____

_____

Posture

In this shade, we are brushing off the blemish of the false priesthood. False priesthood is simply living from a place that produces lack. False priesthood is also misplacement of perspective. This is placing ourselves on a throne when we belong in the servant role or placing ourselves in a servant role when we are called to rise above the fear and take our rightful place.

> *We do not want to place ourselves on stages when we belong in the storehouse stocking our spiritual homes.*

In the same way, we do not want to elongate our creative process because we disqualify ourselves due to our current season. When we are in these places, we can either reach total surrender or hinder what is good.

Here's a challenge: Let go of your plan and perspective so that you *can't* take credit for the product or outcome. Ask:

What does yielding your perspective look like? What will it take for you to take a chance on trusting again? What is something that you can take responsibility for? What role did you play in either the problem or the outcome? When you are chosen by God, *you are royal*, and there is no plan B.

Royalty is not your ability to walk into a room and be the most liked or accredited; it's your ability to walk into a room and be obedient and yielded.

Feeling Unqualified

The beauty in losing our identity is learning the art of yielding our identity. I could stop trying to be someone I thought everyone else wanted me to be and start embracing authenticity. I had *no* desire to be in front of people and be seen. God PLACED that desire inside of me. As a shy, anxious, insecure teen, I just wanted to hide, yet God wanted me to be seen. Who could I become when I came from nothing, was good at nothing, and knew nothing? I was just a girl who lost her dad and was abused, bullied, and confused. Your identity is far beyond what you can see or feel. It's time to relinquish control!

Think and reflect:

What ideas or desires are you holding on tight to?

What control do you struggle to relinquish?

Why do you want control so badly?

Are you desiring this thing because you believe it will fill the broken part of you?

Who do you claim God is to you?

Being royal means being able to understand your Maker and surrender your idea of what life was supposed to look like. When we surrender, we begin to understand what we were made for. When we don't surrender, we do not understand. Surrender doesn't always mean developing; it often means offering. I always want God to have the first of me—the gift is His. This is why the way we live our lives is a result of who we worship.

> Honor the LORD with your wealth and with the firstfruits of all your produce; then your barns will be filled with plenty, and your vats will be bursting with wine. (Proverbs 3:9–10 ESV)

Season 10: White

The Pure in Heart

With no illustrations, no fluff, and no perfection

*P*urity is:

1. Innocence, clean, bright, pure, good
2. Freedom from anything that debases, contaminates, pollutes

Defining Purity

We've talked about it through nine seasons. Purity. What is it? I'd like to define the word that's highly misunderstood yet applicable to the married, unmarried, virgin, non-virgin, raped, abused, and confused. Living a pure lifestyle is God's original design for humanity. Imagine this: we are the "ing," and God is the "ed." We are in process; He is perfect. Everything that you read is constantly evolv*ing*—to new levels, new generations, and new mindsets. He is complete; we are undone. He is the beginning to our end. He is the end to our beginning, so there must be an *intended* way to live that was established before we got here. Since God has already created (past tense), what does creating (present tense) obedience look like for us today?

If purity is to be bright like fire, then we must *burst* with bright light. Purity is vibrancy. If everyone knew you were abstinent, if everyone knew that you were the one that gets around, if *no* one knew you were abstinent, if *no* one knew that you were the one that gets around, none of it would make a difference. Not for you, and not for them. You know why? Because sexual activity is not YOU; it's a status. Sex, in and of itself, is not sin; sin is when we pervert what's good and use perversion to our benefit, making it permissible. Sex is not who you are; it's not an identity. If that were the case, then abuse would mean you lost your virginity, or because you liked it, you sinned. No. Your past sexual history or activity is not what deems you pure or impure. Only God can truly measure the intent of the heart, and we must not abuse the grace of the cross. That means that whether you watch porn, indulge in orgies, have sex with one partner, or are abused or raped, it's all covered by grace. You know how I know? Because I've done it all in my head, in my heart, or in reality at one point or another, and I still live free because the real freedom is not in the status; it is in my devotion, in my repentance, in my pursuit, in my will, in my surrender, and in His grace. When my mom named me Gracelyn, God knew that I would come to meet grace face to face.

Our freedom is unattached from the frequency of the sites we visit or the daydreams that we have about a person. Our freedom is in what we *choose to pursue*. The enemy has tactics to keep you bound by way of deception. What if the impurity or sin was not the act itself but what took place before you got in the bed, before you typed the porn site, before you sent the text, before you cussed them out, *before*. Sexual activity is a result of what you do or don't do based on the knowledge and conviction that you obtain or lack. Sin is produced from a seed planted at an event because of a problem, position, or person. Sin is a result of what happened *before*. In the beginning (before us), there was temptation in the garden of Eden that caused the fall. Temptation has never left; it was present in the beginning, but because of Jesus' death and resurrection, we now have access to a renewed mind and spirit. Jesus did this for us.

> The Word became flesh and made his dwelling among us. We have seen his glory, the glory of the one and only Son, who came from the Father, full of grace and truth. (John testified concerning him. He cried out, saying, "This is the one I spoke about when I said, 'He who comes after me has surpassed me because he was before me.'") Out of his fullness we have all received grace in place of grace already given. For the law was given through Moses; grace and truth came through Jesus Christ. No one has ever seen God, but the one and only Son, who is himself God and is in closest relationship with the Father, has made him known. (John 1:14–18)

> Watch and pray that you may not enter into temptation. The spirit indeed is willing, but the flesh is weak. (Matthew 26:41 ESV)

Lust and the Tension of the Now

I was between two worlds, but apparently, I didn't have a choice as to which one I wanted to live in. My abuser chose for me. I thought maybe I'd have a say in if I wanted it, but pushing her off my body and away from my anatomy wasn't enough. I wasn't sure if this was abuse, seduction, or if there was a difference. It hurt so good until it hurt so bad—until it left a question mark on who I desired. She went to sleep that night. Meanwhile, I'm in deep thought. What just happened to me? Why couldn't I save myself? Why did I like it and hate it? I thought about it every night. It replayed over and over in my head, and I didn't know how to shut off what now turned me on. How do I pull the power from what plugged me in? It was pleasure and pain coming from a broken source. I didn't know if this was love or lust; my pre-teen psyche just couldn't comprehend.

I hadn't watched pornography in two years, but when I wrote this to free people from what held me, I felt like it got me again. Purity is progression, not perfection. If only we could give ourselves and others the same grace that God gives, or at least maybe close to it. The real battle was not in falling; it was in feeling and forgiving. If only I could wrap my head around feeling my frustration and not suppressing it *while* letting go of the timeline of "being clean" for two years. I could then grasp the truth that God doesn't have a timeline. He has grace, love, and mercy, and we have numbers, memories, and shameful nature. Love keeps no record of wrong . . . but *we* do.

From Lust to Love

Some don't date to marry; they date to *feel*. I noticed that I missed dating and my old lifestyle because I missed feeling. Over time, I became numb, and I didn't realize that I desired something from my past because I was desiring a feeling that I missed. What I called love was simply my soul being in tune with what I *felt*. If I had been married then, I would have leaned on my spouse in a way that he would not be able to carry my weight. Co-dependency is just a longing that desires fulfillment from lack. In my first relationship, I laid down my life for my boyfriend, and we told each other that we would die for each other when I didn't realize that I was missing *love*. I carried my cross for my boyfriend because of how it made me *feel*. I gave my life to him because I was ignorant of the love that I really needed. Love was never as loud as this; lust was what I knew. Being driven by lust is a luring and tempting mindset that, if not controlled, has the potential to be damaging and produce a dependency that always thirsts for more.

> Unto the pure all things are pure: but unto them that are defiled and unbelieving is nothing pure; but even their mind and conscience is defiled. (Titus 1:15 KJV)

When we're used to one way of receiving love, we become accustomed to it. Love and lust cannot coexist. There are levels to lust, and there is *one* standard of love.

Feelings or the production of feelings can include sexting, sex, masturbation, kissing, dating, porn, and the list goes on. They all make your body, mind, or soul feel a certain type of way, and the reason you always want more is you haven't found the depth of love you've sought; love has been tainted by lust. This is not limited to singles but also married couples who just don't feel fulfilled.

As people in process, we need to feel, of course, but if we aren't fully affirmed in our adolescence, we must become aware of the lack we may be masking. We tend to fall into worldly temptation because feelings are faster than faith. There's a point where we feel powerless and inferior to our own mindset and decisions that we aren't always ready to give up. Even if, in my weakness, I gave in to temptation today, right now, there is a Son who ever so shines and reminds me that I am a child of God. I pray that He reminds you, too, here and now. Whatever you have or have not done, He is a covenant-keeping God. He will still extend His grace and glory, and He is the only One who can truly measure your heart.

Purity is progression, not perfection. Purification is an ongoing internal cycle that never ends. Cursing, drinking, premarital sex, murder—it's all sin. There are consequences for all, but *Jesus* cleanses us from the weight of it.

Diligence, dedication, and a decision are the ways that purity can help work in your soul's sanctification; are you diligent or disobedient? Is your heart reaching toward heaven, or are your actions leading you and others toward sin? It's all a choice.

Here are your two choices:

- Diligence—remain committed and do not use imperfection as an excuse or way to sin

OR

- Disobedience—rarely/never do what's required but expect blessings

There is a cost. God is not concerned about your consistency in memorizing Scripture or your quotes on social media. He is pursuing the diligent, and it requires something expensive—your heart.

Diligence Diagram

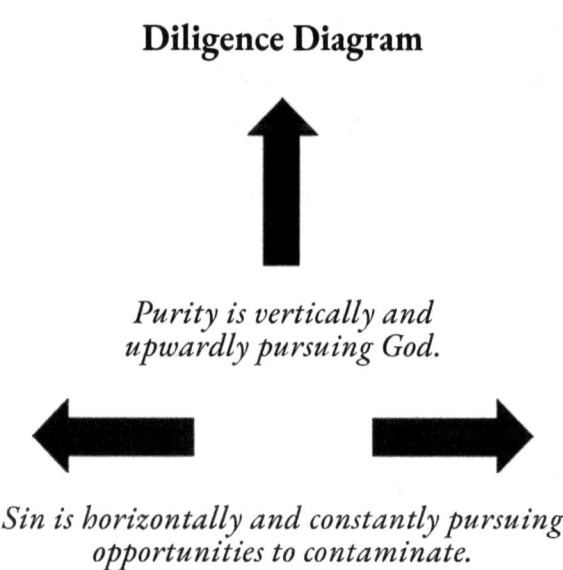

Purity is vertically and upwardly pursuing God.

Sin is horizontally and constantly pursuing opportunities to contaminate.

We must be diligent, vigilant, and aware of the absence of love and the production of sin. Love is a standard; it's upward. Love goes beyond what you think and keeps going. Sin attempts to manipulate what is good in order to contaminate what is pure and righteous. Do not be deceived by what *seems* good.

Purity is vertical; sin is horizontal. Imagine a string going from your heart up to heaven; this is purity. Now imagine a string going from your anger to a neighbor; this is sin.

> We love because he first loved us. If anyone says, "I love God," and hates his brother, he is a liar; for he who does not love his brother whom he has seen cannot love God whom he has not seen. And this commandment we have from him: whoever loves God must also love his brother. (1 John 4:19–21 ESV)

This love is beyond all comprehension. In order to know your standard of love and what love you are to receive, you must know the *source* of love. God does not want us to settle for a lesser love. There may be a different conviction in each of our lives, but we must never live below the calling to be Christ-like. There is a plan that God set in place long before we arrived. This life is not about your expectations but about God's standard, and there is only one: "'Love the Lord your God with all your heart and with all your soul and with all your strength and with all your mind'; and, 'Love your neighbor as yourself'" (Luke 10:27). If you do not embody this Scripture, seek Him deeper to see just what His standard of love looks like, feels like, and sounds like. Then act accordingly—in love.

SHIFT HUMANITY

Standards over Boundaries

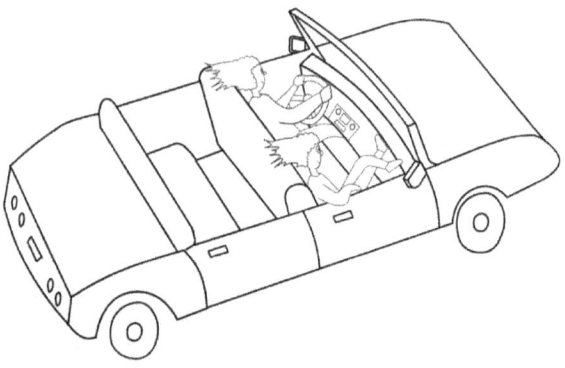

I want to flash back to a car ride with my mom in 2017 when I blurted out so shamelessly: "When I get to college, I'm having sex." Why did I announce this? Because I wanted her to know. In all my mom's peace and understanding, she asked the simple question, "Why?" The only reason I had was because everyone else was doing it, and I'd probably have a boyfriend, so if we love each other, it's happening. I even told her the year that it would happen. I decided it would probably be my junior year. As I kept talking, I pondered the weight of my mom's question. Why? I responded to her a few moments later: "Wait, you're right. I *don't* know why I would give myself to someone who I *think* loves me and *says* they love me but isn't committed to wait for me, work for me, pursue me, and pray for me." I was willing to accept what was easy because I wanted comfort. Why would I give myself to a guy who wasn't *made* for me? Why would I give my energy to a moment that wasn't *designed* for me?

> *Energy exerted wrongfully is still valuable time.*

When we make decisions from our flesh, we can only receive a response from the flesh. We cannot perform fleshly deeds and receive a spiritual response. From that moment, I decided to go against the grain and walk a road that not many were walking. I realized that comfort is casual, and most settle for it. On that same car ride, I told my mom that I was going to wait until marriage to have sex. Two years later, I committed to not kiss until marriage and not even date. I was so passionate yet so confused as to how I even lasted this long, but now I know. I am royalty. Why am I waiting to kiss and have sex? I am waiting to kiss and have sex because I know myself. I know where I'm weak and who I am weak around. I know my triggers. Most importantly, I know my texture, material, and depth.

> *Protection over your heart is more than a boundary; it's a standard.*

Proverbs 4:23 says, "Above all else, guard your heart, for everything you do flows from it."

This is a life that I have chosen to live to protect myself, not only physically, but there is abounding love that I've found in Christ, who loved me enough to be the standard, and you will only catch my eye if you look at the lover of my soul.

> *If you want to pursue me, pursue the One that has been after me since before the foundations of the earth.*

This should be our response. We must become a people that will forfeit comfort for the sake of obedience. Truthfully, I did NOT want to wait. *At all.* I was sexually inclined and burning for pleasure. But I'm saving it all for marriage because my body is a temple, and so is yours.

> *We must stop assuming that things are impossible just because we don't have a desire to try.*

Putting my fantasies aside as a single woman has been a battle. I want sex. I am passionate. I am human. I want to know how it feels with the man God has chosen for me. I desire to feel the butterflies on the carnival date. Faith says I will, but there's still a process.

I have a standard, and I've made a promise. Just as God promises me eternal life for surrendering my life to Him, in exchange, I desire to please Him by keeping my vow. Humbled and alone, I have found my identity in my heavenly Father, who treats me like a queen.

> *Our identity is not about knowing who you are and giving it away; it's knowing whose you are and protecting it.*

Knowing who you are and owning who you are in every arena. I belong to the One who keeps me. When we feel too weak, He's able to take the taste out of your mouth and the knot out of your throat. He comes to arrest lust and seduction. He cuts her neck off so that she can't see. I'm not ashamed. I know what's in me; I know what tingles in every place feel like. I know the worst parts of lust—I was seduced by a woman.

Waiting to have sex until marriage is not a part of my identity. Why? Because if I were to fall into temptation, who would I become? Would my label change to "no longer a virgin" or "failed attempted wait?" No. My label would be Gracelyn Sorrell, the imperfect child who needs God. To know God is to know His desires for us. He knows what our human experience feels like and where lust has the ability to take us, attempting to defeat our true identity. Even *Jesus* was tempted.

> Then Jesus was led up by the Spirit into the wilderness to be tempted by the devil. And after fasting forty days and forty nights, he was hungry. And the tempter came and said to him, "If you are the Son of God, command these stones to become loaves of bread." But he answered, "It is written, 'Man shall not live by bread alone, but by every word that comes from the mouth of God.'" Then the devil took him to the holy city and set him on the pinnacle of the temple and said to him, "If you are the Son of God, throw yourself down, for it is written, 'He will command his angels concerning you,' and 'On their hands they will bear you up, lest you strike your foot against a stone.'" Jesus said to him, "Again it is written, 'You shall not put the Lord your God to the test.'" Again, the devil took him to a very high mountain and showed him all the kingdoms of the world and their glory. And he said to him, "All these I will give you, if you will fall down and worship me." Then Jesus said to him, "Be gone, Satan! For it is written, 'You shall worship the Lord your God and him only shall you serve.'" Then the devil left him, and behold, angels came and were ministering to him. (Matthew 4:1–11 ESV)

Jesus was tempted *first*, which means we have the blueprint for how to walk out a pure, intentional lifestyle.

Application (Purity and Human Nature)

Purity should be the most relevant topic, but *applying* pure principles can be the most irrelevant and unimportant task to us and our human nature. When we live in a world that is saturated with sin and is only escalating in destruction as the days go by, we should question how we can grow in purity as a mom, dad, sister, brother, friend, or leader. The only way we will see God is if we continue to ask Him the hard questions and follow the answer no matter how hard the journey is. Do you think I woke up one morning and said, "Ooo, it is a GOOD day to not have sex," or "Today is a great day to not give into temptation?" NO. I don't wake up a superhero; I wake up in a mortal body—we all do. In the morning and at night, we wake up in a mortal body; we have needs for the day, desires in our brains, and temptation coming at us because of the natural occurrences of the human body. The trick of the enemy is to get you curious mentally so that you can act out physically. So, I stopped flirting with curiosity. Just because your body reacts to something does not mean you have to give it what it wants.

> *An action does not always have to call for a reaction.*

> *Humanity does not leave, but Satan can.*

Our humanity is *real*. People are attracted to people, and people feel they need their outlet, whether it's a release, a hug, a good cry, sex, cuddling, an ice cream date, a walk in the park, late-night car talks, or just the sheer presence of another human.

Our minds are like a garden that we tend. We can tend to what is good, righteous, holy, and pure, and we can dig up, cut out, and pull what is not fertilizing our garden in healthy, fruitful, Christ-like ways. We can cultivate it. It is human to want to entertain sin. It is human to wake up to a temptation. Beyond sexuality, look at how many lies you consume when you open your eyes.

"I'm not good enough."

"I hate my body."

"I'm ugly."

"I don't look like him or her."

Look at Adam and Eve. Because they were tempted, they

sinned and affected EVERYONE after them, and now I have to talk to you about taking your thoughts captive. The beauty in this is that God knows—He knows how you wake up, how you go to sleep, the sounds and motions that trigger you, and even the torment. He knows it all. Imagine a god who is not involved in your humanity. Imagine a god who is careless as you are tempted and tried. That is not the God that I serve. We get to live in partnership with God's presence. Jesus is the greatest example of one who *understands* temptation. I'm grateful to know the God who endured death, sin, and the grave. He was the first to know and conquer the sting of temptation and now gives us the strength to endure.

We *choose* what kind of human we become, and nobody else is to blame. We can either cast down or build up imagination. When you decide that conquering sin is too hard, guess what? It is going to appear too hard. I challenge you to begin speaking to your body—speak to your thoughts, speak to your habits, and tell them that they do not have dominion over you, but the Jesus who died for you has left a Holy Spirit to override and defeat what attempts to attack. Everything led you to this moment; you didn't just wake up and become human. That image from your childhood, that assault, that TV show, those videos—they all planted seeds that attempt to grow.

> *Begin applying the evidence of the cross to your mortal body and watch a sweet transformation take place.*

This is our transformation. You don't have to sit there and accept temptation. You get to decide to conquer it on earth as it is in heaven! I can gladly say that nobody but the Lord has been my keeper spiritually, mentally, emotionally, *and* sexually.

> Psalm 121:5–6 says, "The LORD watches over you—the LORD is your shade at your right hand; the sun will not harm you by day, nor the moon by night."

As He watches over us, may we be watchful and careful in what we pursue and what we *let* pursue us. Regardless of what was felt, we are not our feelings, and we have everything that we need to conquer our sinful nature as we abide in Christ.

> "I am the vine; you are the branches. If you remain in me and I in you, you will bear much fruit; apart from me you can do nothing" (John 15:5).

If you stop resisting God, it will be easier to resist temptation.

God Wants You

As society evolves, so does sin. Our lack of holy fear and reverence causes comfort, which results in impure thoughts or acts. Scripture says,

> "For if we go on sinning deliberately after receiving the knowledge of the truth, there no longer remains a sacrifice for sins, but a fearful expectation of judgment, and a fury of fire that will consume the adversaries" (Hebrews 10:26–27 ESV).

Purity or impurity is not based on the action; it's based on the posture. We must be watchful and ask ourselves: "Where am I? Why am I here? Who said that to me? How did that affect me?" We are not to abstain only from premarital sex but rather from *rebellion*. To the abuser, to the victim, to the virgin, to the fornicator, to the addicted, to the pimp, to the prostitute, to the abandoned, to the bruised, to the touched, to the untouched, to the lonely, to the overlooked, to the poor, to the rich, to the widow, to the mistress, to the orphan, and to every human who is trying to navigate their humanity: Live to be a faithful, obedient vessel. I dedicate this to you with every intention of educating, uplifting, and being a catalyst for your healed mind, body, soul, and spirit.

The goal is not to be accepted by human beings. The goal is to obey the will of God and step into the call for the sake of the cross. We do not exist to gratify our flesh. The goal is heaven, and with everything, with all that we are and all that we have, may we reach out and delight in the graceful, piercing, passionate, transforming, loving, captivating truth that even in these days on earth, we can still receive the goodness of God in the land of the living through the transformation of the Holy Spirit. We can still live the pure lifestyle that was never truly defined accurately by humans. We can start over, we can start today, and we don't have to start the same way by solely counting or marking down the number of times that we fell short. We can allow God to add *reason* to the journey and *grace* for sustaining. God does not keep a record of wrongs. He does not tally up your number of sins per day. He is a gracious Father, measuring our hearts while in pursuit of us. He *wants* us.

We are transformed by love. May you be transformed by enduring love with powerful, sweet conviction in your heart.

Let's become like Jesus because we actually want to, not because we have been manipulated into holiness.

A Humble Humanity

The highlighting you may have done in your Bible or Scripture typed under social media photo captions does not matter if your heart does not highlight the Scripture and your life does not reflect the fruit of what the Bible says. Masking purity does not make you real, just as pursuing a perfect image does not make you perfect. That "holier than thou" statement came from a place of long skirts equating to holiness and short skirts equating to whoredom. Neither is true. A long skirt can be defiled just as the heart of the one with the short skirt can be broken and honest before the Lord. We must discern the difference. It's called righteous judgment.

> "Judge not according to the appearance, but judge righteous judgment" (John 7:24 KJV).

So many are afraid to judge because of reverse condemnation. Personally, if someone's convictions are not yours, you don't stone them; you pray for a change of heart. If someone's convictions are yours, ask God what your position of accountability according to the cross might look like. Once we raise the standard, we no longer become comfortable with compromise. Modesty is a heart posture.

The issue is this is *not* how most judge. So, I apologize for those who called you out of your name, looked at you in disgust, or condemned you based on your outer appearance or actions when they had no position or posture to do so. Righteous judgment should be rooted in love. I have a personal righteous indignation for immodesty and deception. There is a difference between righteous indignation and judging based on your discomfort or disgust. Surprisingly, love corrects, and this means that we have a duty to approach the throne of God, asking to pursue our heart with His transforming love, not transform with the darts that we throw just because we don't agree with what meets the eye. We must repent, and, at the same moment, we must hold to truth. The truth is that none of us *deserve* gentle correction. We all deserve wrath, but because of Jesus, we get grace. I understand grace all too well. I wish I didn't need it, but I cannot hide my humanity. We all have all sorts of sins that are covered by grace. So when you feel like judging someone, ask God to reveal what spirit or experience might be behind that action. Pray for that spirit to be subjected under the cross, and ask Him to correct *you* first.

We live in a culture where it's easy to point out but difficult to point in.

Where is *your* heart? Where are you in your salvation walk?

Social media gives us opportunities to judge without seeing through spiritual eyes but rather carnal eyes because, after all, when we scroll, we see what we feel, but that's invalid. If you look at the speck in someone else's eye, but you have a plank in your own, you are a hypocrite, according to Matthew 7:3–5. You have committed what's like a double homicide. *How could we?* We have all done it. Let's work on discerning the spirit or experience behind a person rather than scanning their faults. Measuring one's acts should be handled biblically and gracefully. "For by the grace given me I say to every one of you: Do not think of yourself more highly than you ought, but rather think of yourself with sober judgment, in accordance with the faith God has distributed to each of you" (Romans 12:3).

The standard that we should hold for others is one that exemplifies that, if not for grace, we, too, would be burned and cast away. We are sinners saved by grace and called to pray sincerely for the salvation of others and for the Lord *Himself* to come and bring judgment. Let's take ourselves off the throne so that the One who knows all can purify, cleanse, separate, and handle humanity according to His will.

If love became the epicenter of our sight, we wouldn't rank ourselves or measure ourselves against one another. If you want to do better in life, do better. If you don't want to do better, don't drag down the one who does want to do better. A neutral attitude and holding yourself accountable is what equates to freedom.

> *Evaluating everything gives us the opportunity to become learners.*

Whether it's an outfit, an attitude, a look, or a smirk, what are you receiving and giving in every single moment and why?

> "People look at the outer appearance, but the LORD looks at the heart" (1 Samuel 16:7).

At the same time, we should never, *ever* become complacent in sin and blame it on the nature of God's grace. You must look at yourself and improve the places that you resist seeing, dealing with, or admitting you have.

In essence, sin is wrongdoing. In your heart of hearts, you know what's wrong. You may not have identified *why* it's wrong, but you may know it's wrong because of that pit in your stomach. Grasping onto the knowledge of why you are who you are gives God space to define what you were created for. This ultimately gives reason as to why you live, and that truth shifts our actions. So, beyond who we are, let's visit the truth of what we were *made* for.

The Journey

Temptation doesn't come with red horns and a scary voice. It comes gently, with patience, and enters wisely, steadily in stealth mode. At sixteen years old, I dedicated myself to saving sex for marriage. At seventeen, I asked God for the desire to wait; I asked for a revelation as to what purity *really* was. Now, here I am in one of the last spectrums of *Shift Humanity*, so my prayer was answered. I say that to say that temptation can be turned to revelation if we're open to the shift.

Purity is not perfection because perfection is not humanly attainable. We live a pure lifestyle to obtain the specific goal of bringing Jesus, the holy, perfect One, into our unholy, imperfect moments—the good, the bad, and the ugly. Let's stop running from Him when we fall short; let's seek Him so that we can approach His throne of grace again and again. Leave shame behind, and enter your next moment with confidence in who you serve. You have this promise: "Blessed are the pure in heart: for they shall see God" (Matthew 5:8 KJV).

Purity and Humanity: What We Were Made For

In doing daily tasks like laundry, work, grocery shopping, handling several situations at once, being tired, eating, showering, and all the in-betweens, I start to think about the pressures and responsibilities that come with living. The days waking up feeling like there's nothing I can offer or the days that I scroll all day looking for the work to finish itself. Even preparing the oatmeal I eat in the morning becomes pressure because I probably shouldn't skip breakfast. I often ponder, "Why do I have to do all these *things*? Why does my stomach need food? Why do my feet have toes? Why does the air have oxygen? What is the meaning of life? *Why am I here?*"

I'm reminded of the time I woke up wanting to go back to sleep because if I woke up, I'd have to figure out why all over again. So, I asked God the question often: What was I created for? Beyond the showers, the cultivation of new and old friendships, or pan-searing the salmon for dinner. It seems like we receive just to let go, we use, then dispose of; we eat, then digest, and still dispose of that. *But what is it all for?* It's all a recyclable question mark that we rarely sit down to get answers to; we spiral into anxiety and depression trying to figure out why it all matters.

The highest form of relevance that we have is in relation to our heavenly Father. Whatever is not done, created, or produced in Him has no clarity. We live, breathe, and have our being to glorify Him, and the beauty is . . . that's enough reason to live. As I live in question and pursuit of my next chapter, I am reminded that the *whole world* is out there—the people, the needs, the systems, the media. I think of how many world functions are "successful" yet producing toxicity. How many systems are controlling and running with ease, and how uninvolved are we because we are focused on the person who didn't text us back? Evil is prospering, and untrue "Christian" narratives are the "new black." What we are called to is beyond measure and restriction. You get to incorporate meaning into every industry that you enter. You're alive to be the light and reflect vibrant colors throughout the many sectors of the world. You are here for a specific, intricate purpose. Watch how you execute your expression because it is changing the world person by person and moment by moment. It's time to generate positive societal impact. It's time to go *Shift Humanity*.

Declare this with me:

I am relevant to this time. I am a piece to the puzzle. I am necessary. I am waking up out of my slumber, and my heart is taking courage. Be not discouraged, my heart; I have a God who created me for such a time as this. I am relevant to this time, which means purity is relevant to this time. I produce purity in the environment that I have been called to, and everything after me and around me is blessed. I was created to be a *Humanity Shifter*. In Jesus' name, Amen.

Final Reflection

I want to remind you of a few things that God said . . .

God said to **occupy**:

> And he called his ten servants, and delivered them ten pounds, and said unto them, Occupy till I come. (Luke 19:13 KJV)

God said that you are more than a **conqueror**:

> No, in all these things we are more than conquerors through him who loved us. (Romans 8:37 ESV)

God said that you can do all things through Christ who **strengthens** you:

> I can do all things through him who strengthens me. (Philippians 4:13 ESV)

God said that He has **never left you** nor forsaken you:

> The Lord himself goes before you and will be with you; he will never leave you nor forsake you. Do not be afraid; do not be discouraged. (Deuteronomy 31:8)

God said that He **knows** you well:

> For you created my inmost being; you knit me together in my mother's womb. I praise you because I am fearfully and wonderfully made; your works are wonderful, I know that full well. My frame was not hidden from you when I was made in the secret place, when I was woven together in the depths of the earth. (Psalm 139:13–15)

God said that He **delights** in you:

> The Lord delights in those who fear him, who put their hope in his unfailing love. (Psalm 147:11)

God said that this pain is **temporary**:

> For our light and momentary troubles are achieving for us an eternal glory that far outweighs them all. So we fix our eyes not on what is seen, but on what is unseen, since what is seen is temporary, but what is unseen is eternal. (2 Corinthians 4:17–18)

God said that this is **not unto death**:

> I shall not die, but live, And declare the works of the LORD. The LORD has chastened me severely, But He has not given me over to death. Open to me the gates of righteousness; I will go through them, And I will praise the LORD. (Psalm 118:17–19 NKJV)

God said that you are a **masterpiece**:

> For we are His workmanship [His own master work, a work of art], created in Christ Jesus [reborn from above—spiritually transformed, renewed, ready to be used] for good works, which God prepared [for us] beforehand [taking paths which He set], so that we would walk in them [living the good life which He prearranged and made ready for us]. (Ephesians 2:10 AMP)

Becoming fixated on a matchless King means giving up your ability to understand. When we are consumed, we give up control.

Consumption allows us to give ourselves over to the One who desires to know us. Notice I didn't say to the One that we know. To give yourself to Yahweh—it's not always going to be when you're in love with Him, and sometimes not even when you really know Him. We give ourselves to God by faith; we trust in the Lord by faith. If you're not in a place where you feel ready, there will never be a better time than today. Being consumed means you finally understand that you need saving.

> If you declare with your mouth, "Jesus is Lord," and believe in your heart that God raised him from the dead, you will be saved. For it is with your heart that you believe and are justified, and it is with your mouth that you profess your faith and are saved. (Romans 10:9–10)

Humanity is waiting for the dynamic change that only you can bring. You're supposed to be here.

— Gracelyn

Acknowledgments

I give unending thanks to the one who wipes my tears, encourages me in my darkest seasons, and cares about my life and well-being. To the one who helps me up when I trip, carries me when I fall, and sits with me in pitch-black seasons. To the one who declared life over me and life more abundantly, the one who paid for my next meal and sent me flowers, candy, and a gift card. To the one who didn't just pass through but remained. To the one who held my hand through heartbreak and sat through the not-so-speedy recovery. To the one who inconvenienced herself to be present. To the one who got on the ground with me and showed me how to stretch out the tension. To the one who reminded me how to breathe. To the one who did not dismiss my emotions but edified me in them. To Mom, thank you for helping me to *Shift Humanity* and for being my first example of a *Humanity Shifter*. To my bonus dad who has stepped in – Thank you. God rewrote my story and I'm so glad you're in it.

Most importantly, I thank God, my Heavenly Father, and my Lord and Savior Jesus Christ, the greatest *Humanity Shifter* of all time. Victory over defeat would not be possible without You. God be glorified. In Jesus' name, Amen.

NOTES

www.ingramcontent.com/pod-product-compliance
Lightning Source LLC
Chambersburg PA
CBHW070615030426
42337CB00020B/3808